Y0-BZV-307

MERE CHRISTIAN

Stories from the Light

MICHAEL COREN

CASTLE QUAY BOOKS
C A N A D A

MERE CHRISTIAN

Copyright © 2002 by Castle Quay Books Canada
All rights reserved
Printed in Canada
International Standard Book Number: 1-894860-02-0

Published by:
Castle Quay Books
1740 Pilgrim's Way, Oakville, Ontario, L6M 1S5
Tel: (416) 573-3249   Fax (519) 748-9835
Email: info@castlequaybooks.com
www.castlequaybooks.com

This book or parts thereof may not be reproduced in any form
without prior written permission of the publisher.

Cover Design by John Cowie - Eye to Eye Design
Proof Reading by Janet Dimond
Printed at Essence Publishing, Belleville, Ontario

National Library of Canada Cataloguing in Publication

Coren, Michael

Mere Christian / Michael Coren.

ISBN 1-894860-02-0

1. Christian life. I. Title.

BV4510.3.C67 2002

248.4

C2002-904510-X

CASTLE QUAY BOOKS
C A N A D A

TO MY FATHER PHILIP COREN (1927-2002)

Table of Contents

INTRODUCTION

*U*sing the title *Mere Christian* is, to say the least, a little impertinent. That great lion of Christian thought and literature, C.S. Lewis, used *Mere Christianity* as the title of arguably the greatest single volume of Christian apologetics ever written. But then he had borrowed it from someone else. I play with his phrase, however, not out of immodesty but out of reverence. Simply, I owe Lewis more than I can ever say. He helped me, and countless others, along that road which ends in the outstretched arms of Jesus Christ.

What I have tried to do in this book is to deliver a series of arguments on subjects that are particularly pertinent to Christian believers. Faith, family, love, relationships, prayer, life and death, human suffering and joy, the reality of Jesus. Anecdotes, memories and stories, combined with facts and analyses. Some, though not all, of the pieces here started life as columns for newspapers and magazines, but I have edited and enlarged them into short essays. Still to the point and readable I hope, but more fleshy and rounded than in their previous life.

I have collected them in various segments and subsections, all of which have a direct link to the Christian world and to Christian thinking. Indeed this is the first time that I have written a book aimed squarely at the Christian market and a Christian audience. Having said that, I hope very much that this book will be read by Christians and non-Christians alike. I have never been a fan of the language and style of the evangelical sub-culture or of any idiom or approach that keeps searchers away from the truth. Thus these essays should stand alone, whether the reader is a believer or not. Atheists are most welcome.

Any failings, of course, are solely my responsibility. But I would be ungrateful and ungracious if I didn't thank the following for their help and inspiration. For those whom I have forgotten, please forgive me. To Bruxy Cavey, Darryl Dash, Tony Campolo, Ravi Zacharias, David Mainse, Larry Willard, Lorna Dueck, Brian Inkster, Alison Hayes, Paul Goodman, Stephen Hayhurst, Nina Cavey, Dave Wilson, Lorrie Goldstein, Doug Koop, Charles Price, Peter Mackintosh thank you so very much. To my wife Bernadette and children Daniel, Lucy, Oliver and Elizabeth I owe the debt of one who learns from those far greater than he could ever be.

To my parents, thank you for giving me foundation, existence and love. To my Father in heaven, forgive me for not loving you enough and thank you for being.

ON FAITH

There are five pieces in this first section, all of which are based around faith, relationships, conversion and the realization that the world only has genuine and ultimate meaning when it is lived through a knowledge of, and love for, God. Some of the essays are autobiographical, others are stories of other people. All are remarkable, but also commonplace. Miracles occur every day, to many people. In fact the miraculous is often ignored or dismissed. Very sad. But then perhaps it is supposed to be that way. Faith is, of course, a sublime paradox.

George

They had trained so very hard for the event. These Olympics were special, which is why they were called The Special Olympics. There were those who mocked the handicapped competitors as not really being athletes, but that was because such critics were not really wise. George in particular had worked every day at his event, the 100 metre sprint. Pouring rain or intense heat, he was at the track every morning.

Not always easy when you are a young man with Down's Syndrome. Any parent of a challenged child, and most challenged men and women, will tell you that it's not so much the disability that causes the problems but the people who discriminate against you for having it.

When he was stared or laughed at, George responded with smiles. Not because he thought this was how he was supposed to behave, but because it was his nature. He could do nothing else. Such a response confused and worried some, but disarmed and charmed most.

The news that he had been selected to run in the games caused George to, quite literally, jump up and down. His parents had seen this many times before. Birthdays, Christmas, someone else in the house receiving good news. Odd, really, that he should be thought of as handicapped when his joy at his and other people's pleasure was so pure, so deep and so genuine.

After what seemed like an endless wait the day of the event arrived. George was awake at dawn, and made sure, to their qualified delight, that his mum and dad were out of bed as well. He had washed himself so clean that he almost seemed to shine. The car journey to the arena was peppered with questions about crowds, running, times and, most poignant of all, whether grandma would be watching.

Grandma had died some years earlier. Hey, George knew this. He merely inquired, eminently reasonably, whether she would be looking down from heaven to see her favourite grandson run. He was told that she would be. And she would.

A few last words of advice, and then out to the starting line. Eight athletes, with George in the middle. Instructions from the starter, and then the lightning blast of the gun. Off they sprang, with George as rapid as any of them. It was as if he could feel the wind lifting him from the ground. But then disaster. His legs seemed to become tangled and before he knew what was happening he had fallen. He screamed.

It only took a moment for the other seven runners to leave him yards behind, but George's scream was so loud that they, and the crowd, all heard. The runners turned their heads back. Then, gradually, all of them stopped running. Instead of continuing on to victory they all turned 'round and walked back to where their fellow athlete had fallen.

George was crying now, and holding his cut knees close to his chest. The runners knelt down, cuddled him, wiped away the grit and blood from his legs, and picked him up. They put their arms 'round him, told him it would be okay. Then they linked arms, all eight, and walked forward. Together in a line, as one person, they crossed the finish line.

The crowd was silent. Then tears could be heard, then a roar of approval and love so loud that people in neighbouring houses came out of their homes to see what had happened. As they crossed the line the runners cheered, and George begun to jump again, to dance at the beauty and the grace of the moment.

His parents cried and held one another very tight, the organizers hurriedly got hold of seven extra gold medals, other athletes ran to the eight heroes and patted them on the back so hard it hurt. Grandma merely smiled along the golden rays of the sun's warm embrace. This was community, this was goodness, this was the way it was supposed to be.

Christ preached community. He spoke time and time again of the need to value the other person, even if that person had done you harm. He taught us that as children of God, created in His image, we are responsible for one another. To turn the other cheek when insulted is very different from the turning away when someone else is hurt.

As for George, he couldn't stop talking about how hard the ground had been when he fell over. "Did you see me fall mum, did you see me fall?" Yes, his mum said. But more important, she had seen him rise. And seen humanity reach for the stars and the genuine love of God lived out amongst the often despised.

If this was community, caring and Christian sacrifice, what is love and faith? Miriam might be able to tell you, and so could her son Simon. This mother and child have very little, not even a husband and father. He was killed in a futile civil war ignored, even encouraged, by the great powers outside of Africa. Food is limited, water is precious, life is cheap.

There are other things that Miriam and Simon lack. It is apparent when this little boy hugs his mother. In his mind his arms are wrapped so firmly around his mother so tight that he fears he might break her. In her heart his mother feels the embrace, and her eyes fill with tears as she does so. Because Simon has no arms. They were blown off just below the shoulder when he bent down to pick up an old tin with which to play, and the tin can turned out to be a land mine.

Miriam cries a lot. Especially when she recalls the night she planned to kill Simon, and then herself. It was all too much. Too much pain, too much despair. Nothing to live for, not even anything to die for. In the end it was the indifference, the stabbing apathy that forced her hand.

She still doesn't quite know why she couldn't complete the act, couldn't continue to hold the pillow over her son's face. She wasn't afraid, and she was going to do it only because she loved him. Then a voice seemed to whisper in her ear. She'd never heard such a beautiful and perfect sound, and the words were clear but, somehow, weren't words at all. There was no command, no order. Just that lovely sound telling her with a pure, clean certainty that this was wrong. She found herself pulling away in horror. Then she threw herself into the floor and cried.

The next morning she woke to find Simon staring at her, smiling as if he had a wonderful secret to share. Miriam found herself smiling back, and felt lighter and freer than she had ever known. Suddenly they both began to giggle, then to laugh. "A beautiful angel came to see me last night mummy," he said. "She played with me with my pillow, and she was gentle and loving and kind. Then she had to go. Because a very kind man put his arms around her, just like I do with you, and told her it was time to leave. I do hope I see her again."

Nothing will make Simon a complete physical being again, at least not on earth. But he has become a complete spiritual being, as has his mother. They know a happiness now that they never before thought possible. They have also shared this joy in their village; seldom by preaching, but usually by witness. In other words, others see such light in these deeply hurt people that they want the same.

Two victims of injustice, war and greed became workers for Jesus Christ and laughing servants of God. The hugs happen more often than ever, and this time nobody cries.

Meeting

 The corner of two of the city's main streets, on one of those hot summer evenings when everything seems right. To my left is a restaurant and outside of it a large pile of garbage bags awaiting the morning's pickup. Because of the heat, and because there is decaying food in the bags, the smell is awful. I move away. As I do, though, I see movement. A rat? Surely not so large. Then one of the bags tips forward and I realize that it is a man. A street person has found a safe sleep by hiding against a wall, surrounded by bags of stinking garbage.

He hides, of course, because street people are regularly beaten up, even beaten to death, just for fun. Nobody really cares, the thugs believe, and everyone knows that the cops don't treat such an assault or death the same way they would an attack on a "normal person."

The man climbs out of the heap, shakes his head and begins to walk in my direction. He is tiny, a shaking mess and mass of skin and bones. There are open, weeping sores on his face, his clothes are so ripped that I can almost see his genitalia, and he stinks of bodily waste. He comes up to me and in a quiet, frightened voice asks me a question. As he does so his whole body shakes and he is too scared to make eye contact.

"Could you, could you, could you spare some money?" I turn round to answer him and this very gesture of contact makes him shrink back further into his hiding place. I respond by asking him a particularly stupid question. I ask if he is hungry. Guess what, chances are he wasn't going to tell me that he had just dined, dined at one of the best places in town and couldn't have eaten another thing.

He says he is hungry. I tell him I'll buy him some food. At which point I begin to walk to the corner store a few yards away so that I, well paid and well fed and one of the world's privileged, can spend a tiny fraction of what I have to fill this guy's belly for a few hours. As I walk I realize that he is following me. Of course he is. As I would him in such a situation. He walks a yard behind me, like some ancient servant in an archaic culture. He does so because he doesn't trust me. People lie to him all the time, and he's hungry and wants this promised food.

As he walks he trembles and chatters. And stinks. The sickening odour of urine, muck and decay. The cologne I am wearing probably cost more money that he will see in a lifetime. And I'm uncomfortable, embarrassed. Don't know what to say, what to do. People are looking around when they smell him, and they're looking at me! Guess what, it's my problem and not his.

We walk into the store. Me with good clothes and good job. Him with ripped pants and nothing.

I take some milk, chips, peanuts, any food that looks vaguely comforting and nourishing. I walk to the counter. He follows. I put the goods down and wait to pay.

The woman working in the store looks pained. There is a tin of fresh-air spray underneath the corner, used after street people come into the store so as to expunge the smell. I don't blame her. I may do the same. She looks at me. Then at him. Then at me. Then again at him. Then at me again. She seems bewildered, even nervous. A pause, and then:

"Are you two, are you, are you together. Are you together?" She was asking, of course, if I was paying for this man who looked as though he had not seen money in a very long time. Were we together? Was I together with this man? Were we together? A very sensible and easy question.

It seemed to take an eternity for the question to register. Only a second of course. But it was as if the whole world and all of its possibilities suddenly flushed and flashed though my mind. I steadied myself. "Yes," I said. "We are together."

Now some of you may be expecting to say that I spoke to the man, told him about Jesus, read him some spiritual laws and that he's now an accountant living in the suburbs. Didn't happen. I don't know what eventually happened to him, don't know whether he is now dead or alive. Frankly, it could be the former. But I do know what happened to me and what is still happening.

The day will come when I will stand. I will be broken, smashed and stinking. The search will be my own sin. The question will be asked, "Are you two together?" Because of my faith in Jesus Christ, because of my certainty that He lived, died and rose again for me and for all of us, the question will be in the affirmative. "Yes," Yeshua will say, "Yes, we are together." And I will have eternal happiness with my Father in heaven.

What, though, of that man whom I may, or may not, see again in heaven. He may well be dead now, and I cannot believe that God would want it that way. Would want someone to fall through the cracks, to live and die alone and in such pitiful circumstances. My guarantee of salvation demands certain things from me. Including the realization that but for the grace of God I could have been that man living in the garbage. Also demands that I do all I can to rectify the situation, then remind a frequently uncaring world that we are all princes.

Conversion

 Why, people ask, do you Christians insist on commemorating the agonizing death on the cross of a man who lived 2000 years ago? We answer that the man who died was the son of God, who died for us. All of us. Then came His resurrection, which is surely now indisputable and proven. The risen Jesus, seen by hundreds of people, who were so convinced of the reality of the empty tomb that they were willing to die themselves, often under torture, with a smile on their face.

Think about it. People die for the wrong reasons, people die for lies that they believe to be truths. But nobody dies for something they know to be a lie. Yet the men and women who were contemporaries of Christ knew Him, dined with Him, laughed with Him, slept next to Him and shared their lives with Him. They were worldly, hardened people. They saw Him die, and these people knew death and what it looked like.

They then saw their friend and teacher alive again. Even put their hands into His wounds. Were they all naïve and foolish people, desperate to escape reality? Not at all. Surely it is those who deny the obvious and the authentic who are the truly naïve and foolish and who run from what is real.

I certainly did for most of my life. Until that night when I sat watching the television, unable to sleep. Nothing on the screen really. Then I found a show hosted by a gentle soul by the name of Terry Winter. He was interviewing an English Christian minister called Roger Simpson.

Nothing the pair said seemed to leave any mark and when I awoke the next day I could remember nothing of the interview. Yet I felt oddly different, even transformed. It was as if I had had a bath that had washed me cleaner than I could ever have imagined.

I'm a cynical, experienced person, I thought, and this was just a passing phase, a case of physiology playing a trick. There was something else, however. I knew as sure as I knew my face that this Roger Simpson was a close friend of a friend of mine, a Baptist minister named Justin Dennison. I felt as if they were almost brothers.

This certainty ached away at me until, feeling a little foolish, I telephoned Justin to ask him. He was out but his wife Sue was in. I told her about seeing Simpson on the television, but not about my strangely changed state.

There was a long pause. "Twenty years ago at the coffee bar of the University of London in Britain," she said. "Well, twenty years ago that man Roger Simpson converted Justin to Christianity." I felt a warmth swim through my body, and thought I was going to cry.

My sense of newness increased, my attitudes towards people, towards everything, began to change. I was scared. Life was good and I didn't want any changes thank you very much. Finally the pull was too strong. The urge to take that forgotten old Bible down from the shelf and read it. The need to, yes, the need to pray.

To pray! The man must be crazy. I suppose I felt that way myself. I was embarrassed, frightened, confused. But prayer did happen, questions were asked, answers given, arguments had. This God I had found—or had He found me?—was not some Disney creation but a father who wanted my best.

I went to see a minister, took instruction, was baptized. The Sunday morning that it happened the church was full of people I had never met but who had come along especially. I asked them why. "We've been praying for you," they all said. Hundreds of people, familiar with me through my broadcasting, had decided to pray. Churches, groups, individuals. It is, I now know, frequently the case when people suddenly find themselves submerged in the truth of the Christian faith. Thank God for them, thank God for God.

I subsequently met Terry Winter, and we became friends. He had seen God work in these ways many times, and my conversion did not come as a particular surprise to him. I'd liked to have got to know Terry on an even deeper level, but only a couple of years after his and my miracle he died. When I heard the news I went to sit in that same room where I watched Terry on that special evening.

I switched the television on, for some background comfort. And there on the screen was Terry, hosting a show that had been recorded long ago. I felt myself choking up a little as I watched him. Then the camera pulled back to reveal that he was conducting an interview. With a man called Roger Simpson. Was it Terry playing a joke on me from above, or God reminding me of His limitless power and love. Either way, I am so very, very grateful.

Forgiveness

The following is one of the most significant stories I have ever heard. If its moral and morals were followed to a lesser or greater extent by the world's governments, leaders, businesses and citizens the entire universe would change immediately, and change for the better.

It was 1974 in Miami, only a few days before Christmas. A ten-year-old boy named Chris Carrier stepped off the school bus, his head filled with thoughts of the presents he was going to receive from his parents. Or maybe, just maybe, from Santa Claus. As the small, trusting boy walked toward his home a man approached him.

"We're arranging a surprise for your dad," he said. "Could you come with me and help?"

Chris loved his dad. He got into the truck with the nice man. After a few minutes of driving the man told Chris he had to look at the map and check directions. Chris nodded his head. And then, suddenly, Chris was on his back and the man was on top of him, slashing at him with an ice-pick. The thrusts did not hurt as much as shock the boy. The same questions, drenched in terror, smashed into his mind. Why was this happening, what did the man want, where is my dad?

As suddenly as the attack started it stopped. Silence. The man seemed almost apologetic, and then drove on until he and the fear-frozen child reached the Everglades.

"Get out of the truck and I'll call your father and tell him where you are," said the man. The boy got out, walked a few yards and then sat down on a rock.

The man followed, then turned away. As he did there was the loudest crack the boy had ever heard. And then blackness.

Chris Carrier had been shot through the head. The bullet entered his right temple and exited through his left, leaving him blind in one eye. Dazed and semi-conscious, this starving, bleeding little boy wandered around in the wilderness for almost a week. It was on Boxing Day that he was found, 120 km from his home, and returned to his father. It was, of course, a miracle that Carrier survived. The medics found that not only was the boy shot and stabbed but his body was also covered with cigarette burns. The police had a suspect but did not have proof. They believed that the abduction, torture and attempted murder was committed by someone who had worked as a nurse for Chris Carrier's aged uncle but had been fired for drinking. The case was forgotten and Carrier learned to live with the injuries and restore his life.

The scene moves to 1996 and Chris Carrier is a thirty-two-year-old bookstore owner, married with two children and very happy. Suddenly he receives a telephone call from a police officer who worked on the case two decades ago and has never quite let go. He explains that the man has been found and has confessed to his crimes on tape. He is in a North Miami Beach nursing home, blind and wasted. A pathetic wreck of a man. His name is David McAllister and he is 77. He will not be charged because of the statute of limitations.

Chris Carrier drives to the nursing home, gets out of his car and walks to the room of his persecutor. He stops. Then enters.

"I am the boy you tried to kill," he says. The man says nothing. Then a pause. Then this from Chris Carrier: "I forgive you."

And he has and he does. He visits David McAllister every day, cares for him and reads him the Bible.

"I have everything, he has nothing," says Carrier. "I no longer see the man who hurt me, just a figure near death who has nobody."

So what are we to make of this? Simple. Justice is paramount, but in a world where so many of our policies and actions are infected by violence we need to hold up Chris Carrier as a torch of inspiration. "As we forgive those who trespass against us." Not new, but still revolutionary.

Prayer

My sister Stephanie is six years older than me and lives in Britain. We never really got on. I wish it was otherwise, but there we are. We simply never got on. We argued. A lot. Steph also argued with my parents. A lot.

Steph had a daughter, Tessa, but her marriage broke down after a few years and the family tensions grew even worse. After the collapse she had some dreadful rows with me and with our parents. Until after one particularly venomous episode she cut off all contact. Neither she nor her daughter, whom my parents had partly raised, would speak to any of us again.

This was all some years ago and in the meantime I married a Canadian and went to live in Toronto. So it wasn't so bad for me, three thousand miles away from the mess. But it was hell for my parents. Steph got married again and had a second child. Now there were two grandchildren living in Britain and mum and dad could see neither of them. One of them they had never seen at all.

As the years went by the tears dried up and a dark resignation replaced the feverish anguish that had been so difficult to tolerate. A scab formed over the wound. I had tried to make contact with Steph but I didn't even know her new married name. Hard to trace someone without their name. We didn't even know in which town she lived.

Five years ago I became a Christian. Which means I pray. Have to, want to. It's a conversation with my maker, a process partly of speaking but mostly of listening. I rarely pray for tangibles, although I am fully aware that all prayers are answered, even if the answer is sometimes in the negative.

But one day for some reason I felt the need to ask God to repair the bloody tear between my parents and my sister. Don't know why, just knew that I had to ask. Only a short plea. Then I almost forgot about it.

A week later the telephone rings. It's mum, in her wonderful cockney accent that makes me feel warm and safe. "Mike," she says. "You're not going to believe this. I've got a letter here from Stephanie." A long pause. "She says she wants to make up, to meet."

I listen, hardly registering what is being said. "I don't know what to do," she continues. "I'm frightened of starting all the pain again."

My sister has not spoken to my parents in fifteen years. Suddenly I pray for a resolution. My mother receives a letter from my sister four days later, meaning that she almost certainly wrote it the same day that I asked for help. This is strange, this is frightening, this is remarkable.

There is a phone number on the letter. I call it. A man answers. "Is Steph there?" I ask. He wants to know who it is. I tell him. I then hear him tell Stephanie and I hear her saying my name over and over again, as though if she stops I will no longer be there. She is crying, almost hysterically.

She comes to the phone and in between gulps for air she asks me why I didn't make contact earlier. I tell her I didn't know how to. Why, I respond, didn't she contact me? Because, she explains, she kept hearing that we all hated her. When I ask her who said this she can't remember, almost as though the thought was implanted.

I then ask why she decided to break the silence. "Because I heard that dad was very ill and I just couldn't have lived with myself if I hadn't spoken to him." At this point I choke a little. "But Steph, he's fine. He's not ill at all." Again, a thought implanted. This time from an entirely different source.

We chat, we laugh, we cry. Then I say to her that I must reveal something that is very important, something that has changed my life forever. I tell her that on a specific date some years ago I became a Christian. She doesn't answer at first. Then she asks me to repeat the date. I feel a warmth, a sensation that is real yet beyond detailed description. "Mike," she says, her voice shaking. "So did I. Oh my God, so did I."

Mum, Dad, Steph and her husband John, Tessa and little Katie went on vacation to Spain together. They had a wonderful time. And they weren't the only ones smiling. When my dad had a stroke a few months later Steph was there to take care of him. God listens, it is we who are hard of hearing.

ON FAMILY

I have tried to emphasize in all of my Christian writings the absolute need for relationships, and that at its best family is the perfect example of the Godly relationship. Sadly, family can also be the venue for terrible abuse and sadness. However we must not drown in the negative but swim like champions in the positive. Love, love and love again. No Christian can tire of saying the word, living the meaning of it and shouting it to the skies.

I'm lucky to have known love all of my life. In that love I have seen God, sometimes in a context and with a face that might shock some believers and make them feel acutely uncomfortable. My grandpa, my mum's father, was a tough, hard man but one who knew how to love from the bottom of his heart, with all of the beauty of his heart. I wrote of his passing.

Grandpa

There was no obituary of course, no news. The death was private and so was the life. What commemorations there were came in the local pubs amongst his friends in the lyrical tradition of London English that Charles Dickens almost captured.

I speak of the death of my grandpa. He was eighty-nine, it was time. He would have been the first to say so. Blind, unable to walk, a shell of the great man who was. What a lark, he would have said. That great, untamed, kind, strong, wise, gentle man.

He worked at many jobs, never settled for one and never made much money. He and his wife were cockneys and they would have had it no other way. His life was interrupted in 1939 when His Majesty gave him a gun and told him to kill the nation's enemies. He must have been quite good at it, because he survived for six years. He didn't talk very often about his time in North Africa or Italy and never, ever boasted about it.

If the war arose in conversation it was usually the subject of mockery. "Me a soldier? You must be kidding." And he would tell us jokes about stupid officers. "The Krauts? Well, we hated 'em. But I tell you, we respected them as well." Then he stopped. I knew he didn't want to say any more. Yet my mum remembered that every time he came home on leave he had another stripe on his arm.

One year we managed to take him on holiday to Italy and we surprised him with a trip to a southern battlefield. Mum told me that I should leave him alone for a while, but after a few minutes I went looking for him. I saw him, but he didn't see me. I was so shocked. He was kneeling by a wall with some flowers around it and looking at a photograph held in his large, hairy hand. And he was crying. My Grandpa was crying.

Then one day I was looking in his bedroom for a watch he had lost and I found his medals, tucked away. So many of them. I was fascinated by the different colours and the accompanying letters speaking of courage and honour. I supposed at the time that he had misplaced them, just as he had his watch.

He gave me an allowance every Wednesday afternoon when I was small. Sixpence. Worth nothing now, worth little then. It always seemed more important to him than it was to me. It used to confuse me, embarrass me. But I know now just how little money he had and just how reluctant he was to accept charity. Sixpence. A million dollars.

His home overlooked and overheard the railway track and when I slept on the sofa in his living room I was kept awake by trains making their way to parts of the world I had never seen. Adventurous places to me, small industrial towns in reality. But in his home everything seemed exciting, anything possible.

A quarter of a century later my mother telephones to tell me the news. She isn't crying but she has been. She explains that her dad has left me a note and a small box. The note says: "You've never seen these before Mike, so here they are now. Not much, but all for you. Just put them away somewhere, safe keeping. They don't matter. You know I'll love you forever, Grandpa." They were his medals.

Dad

 My mum telephoned me from England. I knew, I just knew. "I've got some bad news for you," she said, beginning to cry. "Dad has had a very bad stroke." I was at the hospital within twenty-four hours.

There he was. Confused, broken, unable to speak. My dad, swathed in those pungent, antiseptic hospital odors. Odd how smells provoke memory. I remembered the same smells from when he would wash his hands after work and before dinner, trying to remove the ground-in dirt and oil from his calloused hands.

His skin was always so tough. I can still recall the scraping sound of the razor on his evening stubble, still see the darkness of the water in the basin after he had cleaned his face. Like yesterday, like now.

I would stand next to him as he washed and he would chat away, telling me tales of his own childhood and letting little drops of moral tuition fall into my lap. Simple, and quite marvelous. "A promise is a promise." It was. He never broke one. He was my father.

He drove a London black taxi for more than forty years.

It was a job that attracted waves of poor young men after the Second World War, a job that paid a decent wage if you were willing to work a seventy-hour week and not complain or give up.

When I was small and we were driving back from soccer matches he would sometimes pick people up who were hailing cabs along the way. He wasn't supposed to, not with me there. But I was six or seven and sat in the hollow space next to the driver's seat where the luggage was stored and where he had placed a special little seat. I was barely noticed.

I could never understand why the passengers treated him with such contempt, such patronizing disregard. He was "cabby" and "driver" and "you!" No he wasn't, he was my dad. But he smiled and said nothing and did his job. They weren't good enough to walk in his shadow. I knew that, and he knew I knew that. Which is what really mattered.

And then he told me more stories from his past, such as about the times he boxed for the RAF. Oh, the pride. And about how his German cousin had gone back to Berlin in the 1930s to rescue his family. The family did not escape and the cousin never came back. A long time ago, said my father, and not for you to worry about. He winked, a wink full of confidence. Never again, he said. I believed him. He was my father.

He always looked so strong, so able to protect me, so powerful. Powerful enough to cry when he felt the need. I heard him weep when my grandmother died. Confusing. How should I react, what should I do? Just be there, as he was for me. He came into my room, saw the fear on my face and recited a short prayer with me for my grandma. He kissed me, held my hand and then drove me to school before putting in his ten hours. No grumbles, no moans. Of course not. He was my father.

I remember his sheer joy when I went to university, the first in the family to do so. Of course he took too many photographs when I graduated and of course he didn't understand the Latin that was spoken before the meal. Who cares? His wisdom was born long before the Romans imposed their language on the world.

He felt a little out of place, but all that concerned this working man in a smart suit was that his son would not follow in his footsteps. "Do you know why I work such long hours?" he would ask me. "So that you won't have to push a cab around and tip your hat to everybody." Then he'd pause. "So that you won't have to." Not said with bitterness but with resolution. There is dignity in labour, he told me, but shame in sloth.

He didn't come on vacation with us to the English coast very often, just didn't have the money. He stayed behind, ate his cheese sandwiches when he got home, and worked. We'd telephone him and tell him we loved him. He already knew. When my first child, Daniel, was born my dad said little. Just sat and stared and smiled. A circle had been completed, a story had been told, a great knight had won his battles. He spoke through his eyes. And what eloquence he had.

What eloquence he still has. As I sit by his bed and hold his hand I see the frustration in his eyes. He has, I suppose, become a child again. The doctors explain that there isn't really very much hope. So we sit and watch and listen and love. He sits up in his bed, the cuts around his face wear he fell still visible, the IV in his arm, and his eyes nowhere. He wears those ridiculous hospital pyjamas that are always a size too small. Oh dad, what have they done to you?

And then the doors of the ward open. It's my sister, Stephanie, with her husband John and their children Tessa and Katie. Three of them walk in, faces grim and grey. But not all of them. Katie is different. This eight-year-old little girl doesn't walk in, she skips. In fact she dances, all the way to the side of her grandpa's bed.

You see, Katie is what is known as handicapped. An odd description really, in that in my experience those with most moral, emotional and spiritual handicaps are the people we generally regard as being able-bodied. Katie was a very premature baby, had two strokes herself when she was tiny, and is now autistic. Actually the correct term is "a person with autism." But I find that semantics are not the issue.

Katie stands by the bed, and then jumps onto it. In a British hospital. The country might have changed, but not that much. This is almost a criminal offense. We say nothing, not sure of what to do. Then it gets worse. Katie pulls back the blankets and slides inside next to her grandpa. At this point we expect the Queen to arrive and give us all a good telling off.

But Katie hasn't finished yet. She puts her arms around my father, and she falls asleep. We are silent. We just watch. Then, then, then. Then for the first time in two days my father shows emotion. Pause. For the first time in more than 48 hours my father shows emotion.

He cries.

My father cries. Weeps. Tears bisect his unshaved cheeks and he cries like a baby. We panic like babies. We call for the doctor, shout for the nurses. This wasn't meant to happen. What is going on here? The doctor arrives and, bless him, he didn't mean to say what he did. "Oh my, I didn't expect this. What happened? This is miraculous!"

He was right. It was. A miracle had taken place. Not performed by me or any of the other educated, respected people in that hospital, not by anyone with a theological degree or medical training. But by a despised little girl whose parents had been advised to leave their church because, "Katie is a bit noisy for some of the people here."

Katie performed a miracle that day. In fact Katie was Jesus Christ that day. Because she gave the gift of unconditional love. She didn't judge the situation, judge the person, judge anything. She reached out in love, of love, with love. We with our university degrees, polished manners and social acceptance fumbled around looking for answers. Katie didn't even have to ask the question. She merely lived the example of Yeshua.

Love God and love your neighbour as yourself. Simple really, but how often we try to hide that truth in a forest of thorny bushes. Instead of love we look to fear, order, rules and prohibitions. All have their place, but at the heart must be love.

I didn't fly 3000 miles in the middle of the night because I feared my father and because I wanted to obey my father or because I thought that the law demanded it. I did so because I loved him. I do my best to live according to God's will not because I fear Him but because I love Him.

We obey God, lead life according to how He wants, do His will, because we love Him. The love must come first, and as an inevitable consequence an obedient life will follow. Rules and order without love is legalism. And legalism gives us no right, nor ability or power for that matter, to change the world and build the kingdom. It is something that Katie knows very well. Pray all of us will listen to her teaching.

A postscript. At the very time of finishing this book my father died. As I sit here typing these words there are tears clouding my eyes. Emotions are flooding through my body, and they are not the ones I expected. Grief of course, but also anger and guilt. Anger that he didn't have longer and guilt that I didn't love and respect him enough. But does any son love and respect his father enough? Do we love and respect and love God enough?

Dad had more than two years of life after his first stroke, and in that time I brought my parents over from Britain to Canada for a visit. Thank God I did. They saw me record my television show, saw where their grandchildren went to school, saw Lucy score the best goal in soccer in history. Well, to them it was. At this point all I can do is put my faith in the great father of us all in heaven and rely on His peace. Good night dad, I love you.

Lucy

 My Lucy was three-years-old and has never been to live theatre before. She counts down the days, and when the morning of the long-awaited evening breaks, she asks me, as she crawls from her bed and while her eyes are still slits in her brown, puckish face, "Are we going now?" Soon, I reply. Very soon.

She is ready two hours before we have to leave. Party dress, party shoes, party coat, party smile. But first there is dinner with dad. One of the jewels in the crown of infancy is how children are so impressed with what are really quite commonplace things. The extraordinary within the ordinary. A hot dog and a few fries are suddenly transformed into a culinary delight.

Then off to the theatre. And a miracle happens. In that twilight of expectation as the curtain begins to rise, my daughter's eyes become accustomed to what is before her. She gasps, and says, "They're real people. Daddy, they're real people." This tot accustomed to television and cinema has suddenly felt a much more delicious breeze than has ever blown from any electronic media.

From the opening stanzas of Tchaikovsky's genius this child of mine is embraced by the experience. She claps with the rest of the audience at the end of every scene. No prompting, no self-consciousness. Goodness, she can barely sit still. The intermission comes. "Why dad, why?"

Then the second half. That nasty mouse bullies his way across the stage but Lucy isn't scared. Hey, brave as well as brilliant. As for me, although I have seen this ballet many times I am now seeing it through new, better eyes. I am, as it were, seeing it for the very first time.

We leave the theatre and drive home. My wife and son are waiting up for us. Lucy rushes into the house and her mum asks her all about it. Did they wear costumes? "No," says Lucy, "they were real." But then the smile begins to fade, and suddenly this miniature in a floral dress is sobbing uncontrollably, hugging me with all the strength in her tiny body. She is shaking.

I ask her what the matter can be. At first she says she has a tummy-ache, that constant explanation for tears and temper offered by kids the world over. Then she pauses, and in-between gulps of air enlightens her stupid father as to why she is so upset.

"When I take my party dress off (tears), when I take it off and put away my special shoes (tears), then, then it will be over (tears), the ballet will be all over, the magic will end," and she buries her head in my chest in a sea of weeping.

I hold her so close, trying to fold her into me and take away the pain. I tell her that there will be more ballets, more dinners, more dressing up, more fun. "There's something else Lucy," I say. "I promise you from the bottom of my heart my darling, with everything I have and everything I am, that the magic will never ever end. Lucy my love, the magic continues for ever."

She looks up at me, head to the side, the crying milder. Really daddy, do you really mean that? "Oh yes, oh yes, oh so very much yes." And through the tears and the redness comes a smile, deep and broad enough to conquer an empire.

The love between fathers and daughters is a type of dance in itself. A dance of joy that also goes on forever. Lucy is a young lady now, devouring books, watching movies, playing with school friends, laughing at her dad and, yes, going to the live theatre. As for her daft old father, he still dances with his daughter. Even when she doesn't know it.

If a flawed, sinning and broken man such as myself can feel such love for a child, we can only marvel at what God, who is love, feels for us. He has tried so many ways, for so very long, to get us into heaven to join Him. To be with our Father. Finally He sent His one and only son, to die for us. I suppose that in a way God's relationship with His creatures, His loved children, is in itself a dance. God's dance. Yes, God's perfect and never ending dance.

ON LIFE

I have argued for some time that we as Christians tend to be overly selective in the battles which we fight. We tend to be, shall we say, a little too discerning in what constitutes valid areas of moral and Biblical conflict. As such we isolate ourselves, and more importantly isolate Jesus. Having said this, it does not mean that the issues of sexuality, family and life are not important. On the contrary. They are at the very center of the struggle for human dignity and God's truth.

I have included three pieces I wrote about euthanasia and two that I wrote about the unborn. Here, by the way, we are forming alliances with non-Christian and non-faith groups, and this is vital. Advocates for the mentally and physically challenged, groups representing the aged community, medical ethicists and many others are realizing that we may not be the extremists and the blockheads written of in the media.

Euthanasia

 We have heard a great deal recently about the rights of the terminally ill to be assisted to die. Arguments in favour of what is known as euthanasia or, the ultimate oxymoron, compassionate homicide abound in the mainstream media. The points are compelling, because pain and suffering are such gruesome debaters. But there is more, much more, to the euthanasia controversy than feelings, however deep and heartfelt they may be.

Though my heart goes out to anyone with a dying relative, I cannot support a person's right to commit suicide or be helped into that sleep of death by someone who assumes to know best. Of course it is excruciating to face someone in such a position and remain steadfast in your argument, but nobody ever said that being on the side of the angels would always be easy.

Surely the very last people who can make calm and balanced decisions about life and death are those who are in pain and those who are close to them. Emotion and anguish are powerful factors and they make for a gripping story. But by their very nature they obscure clear thought.

Nor are dying or seriously ill people insular beings, somehow cut off from outside influence. They think they know that "it would be so much easier for the kids if they didn't have to come all this way all the time and see me like this." They think they know that "I can't serve any real purpose any more. I've had a good life anyway."

Such thoughts do not make for objective decisions. And, anyway, even the state does not believe that our lives are own. Wear those safety belts in the car, give up smoking, put on the bike helmet. Why? Because your life is worth preserving, even if you don't think so.

Then we take a look at countries where euthanasia is permitted, such as the Netherlands. Last year 10,000 "Don't Kill Me" cards were issued because so many doctors had been, shall we say, a little liberal in their decisions about who should live and who die. In one case a Roman Catholic nun, a strong opponent of so-called mercy killing, became a victim of the practice. She had obviously not given her consent.

This was legal murder, and the case is far from unique. In Holland up to a third of the victims of euthanasia are killed without their or their family's consent being given. The last word, though, goes to a little boy who knew of what he spoke.

"My name is Teague. I am 11 years old, and have really severe cerebral palsy. I feel very strongly that all children are valuable, and deserve to live full and complete lives.

"I have a friend who had cerebral palsy, and he decided life was too hard and too painful. So he really let himself die. I knew he was leaving this world and letting himself dwell in the spirit world. I told him that I understood that the spiritual world was really compelling, but that life was worth fighting for.

"I had to fight to live when I was very sick. The doctors said I wouldn't live long, but I knew I had so much to accomplish still. I had to fight pain all the time. When I was little, life was pain. I couldn't remember no pain. My foster mom, Cara, helped me to learn to manage and control my pain. Now my life is so full of joy.

"There isn't enough time in the day for me to learn and experience all I wish to. I have a family and many friends who love me. I have a world of knowledge to discover. I have so much to give.

"I can't walk or talk or feed myself. But I am not 'suffering from cerebral palsy.' I use a wheelchair, but I am not 'confined to a wheelchair'. I have pain, but I do not need to be 'put out of my misery'.

"My body is not my enemy. It is that which allows me to enjoy Mozart, experience Shakespeare, savour a feast and cuddle my mom. Life is a precious gift. My life is going to be astounding." It was. Teague died, naturally, in the summer of 1995.

No matter how difficult the case, life is not ours to give and not ours to take. As for those reading this who are in such a situation, please forgive my impertinence.

Karen

Karen Shoffstall is dead. She was young, she was pretty, she had so much to live for. But she is dead. At the age of 30 the Ontario native was diagnosed as suffering from multiple sclerosis. The illness is a terrible one, but there are numerous people who live with it for many years, enjoying a fine quality of life.

Such seemed to be the case with Karen Shoffstall. She took vacations, had fun, relished the opportunities that life offered. Yet she had been for some years what her mother describes as "not mentally ill but mentally unstable." She would sometimes fantasize, perhaps tells lies, concoct stories that were not true.

When MS smashed its ugly way into her life Karen would experience bouts of terrible doubt, convinced she was about to lose her job, her friends and her quality of life.

All of this is a far from untypical experience for someone with a profoundly serious medical condition and something with which a counsellor or therapist could deal. But Karen didn't do this. Instead of lifting her head up to the light, she lowered it to the darkness. She made the terrible mistake of writing to Dr. Jack Kevorkian.

The man who has transformed the horror of suicide into a grotesque cult quickly responded. He met the confused Karen in a suburban Detroit hotel room with one of his aides. Shortly afterward the 34-year-old woman was dead, knocked unconscious by an enormous dose of barbiturates, and then killed by potassium chloride.

Kevorkian claims he has a long and extensive list of requirements before he will engage in his grisly trade and that assisted suicide can only occur when the person requesting such a thing is truly in agony and genuinely understand what she wants.

Karen was not, did not. She seldom used a wheelchair. She did not even use a cane very often, and as a trained nurse knew that while MS is chronic, it needn't be disabling. But she was so scared.

"Oh yes, oh yes, so very, very scared," explained her sister, Tina, who lives in Guelph. "She was terrified of what might happen and this was taken as a sign that she didn't want to live any more." A pause for anger as well as grief. "Maybe she did claim that she wanted to die, but was this a decision made sanely and with thought? Not at all. And as for it being her decision and affecting only herself, I wish you could have some idea of what this has done to her family, to her mother." And she points to a quiet, obviously still shaken woman sitting in the corner of the room. A woman who is confused and utterly broken.

"I just know she did not realize what she was getting into, did not understand she was creating horrors in her mind that were not really there," says Karen's mum, a brave and extraordinary person whose wounds are so deep as to be almost visible. "We would always have been there for her." Which poses the question of what we now sometimes refer to as "compassionate homicide" is all about. The last person who can make a clear, cogent decision about the future, about his or her very life, is a person in profound fear. Pain and the anticipation of pain produce such a fear. Then there are the social pressures.

Karen was afraid of losing her lifestyle, an attractive Manhattan lifestyle that we see lionized on television and in the movies. She believed that anything else was simply not worth having. How terribly and, as it turned out, fatally wrong.

Death provoked by a lowering of social expectations is almost too repugnant to contemplate. We also have to consider the implicit beliefs of the old or sick. "I know it would be easier financially for the family if I wasn't here ... it's such a long way for them to come every week and the grandchildren don't like it ... I've had a good life and the insurance will be so helpful for them ... I just don't fit in."

I just don't fit in. The chilling death-rattle exploited by the social engineers. The plea of despair screamed by Karen Shoffstall that fell on the deaf ears of a so-called doctor and his cadaverous sidekick in Detroit, Michigan.

Karen's case is not unique. But Karen was. And for her mother and sister there will never be another. God have mercy on her. And God have mercy, and righteous judgement, on Jack Kevorkian.

Proposal

 I consider the following to be merely a modest proposal. It is this. Let us kill all able-bodied people. Let us murder the healthy and slaughter the fit. Let us sterilize the ones we don't kill so they cannot procreate and, as a pre-emptive strike, abort them in the womb for the sakes of their parents and of greater society.

Now let me make myself completely clear here. I do not for one moment mean we should be sadistic or cruel in our actions, although killing is never completely clean or painless. But whenever possible what some have defined as "compassionate murder" should involve the least amount of agony possible for those we kill. They are not, after all, animals. Then again, animals apparently have rights these days and enjoy the protection of celebrities and the support of extremely well-financed pressure groups. We have to be coldly realistic. Many, if not most, of these able-bodied people lead futile, vacuous lives with little point and less hope. They might not actually ask us to end their sordid little existences, but that is hardly the point. Their suffering is obvious and they are, after all, nothing at all like us. It is for their own good. Many of them complain about their lot in life and about how hard it is to keep going every day. Goodness me, it's not as though any able-bodied person is ever going to be famous and brilliant, like a Stephen Hawking or someone.

Apart from anything else, the healthy and the fit are extremely expensive to maintain and are prone to be dirty, parasitic and even criminal. We shouldn't forget that Stalin was able-bodied, as were Hitler, Mao, Ivan the Terrible, Attila the Hun and most of the great evil doers of history. In fact, it is a proven point that almost every murderer, rapist, pimp, fraud, abuser and thief is able-bodied.

Obviously, I have heard the arguments from those lunatics and fanatics who moan about how life is sacred, how the so-called culture of death is so pervasive and how we have no right to play God.

I've heard them say able-bodied people are frightened to go to sleep at night because they are terrified of what might be done to them. I've also heard the story about that tiny able-bodied boy who looked up at his mother after some court decision and said, "I know I'm a lot of trouble mummy but I'll try to be better in the future. Please don't kill me. Please let me live."

All these arguments in favor of the able-bodied are nothing more than sentimentality and extremism. I mean, who knows what is best for the able-bodied, young and old —us or them? The question is rhetorical, the answer is obvious. We're trying to build a New Jerusalem here. Okay, it might sometimes look more like the old Gaza Strip, but nobody said a perfect society would be easy to create. We must also make sure our judges and lawyers are willing to change the fundamentals of the legal system and the nature of justice so any of us who do kill able-bodied people serve only a few months in prison for what we do, followed by a few more watching television in the comfort of our own homes. When judges do treat murder as if it were a speeding offence we must praise them for being brave and compassionate. This shouldn't be difficult, as so many people in the media are already onside. Nor must juries contain any able-bodied members, otherwise they might not understand our intentions, might empathize with the able-bodied and might even call us murderers and make us serve 10 years in prison or something ridiculous like that. Natural law must be ignored and we must be protected against what we like to describe as cruel and unusual punishment.

It might sound harsh but it comes down to this. Kill, kill, kill them, for goodness sake. There are many precedents in our history. Just a proposal. And a modest one at that.

Unborn

 As I have written elsewhere, contemporary Christians have to be holistic in their politics. That is, we cannot satisfy ourselves with being passionate on only one or two issues and being indifferent to the rest. Christ's example teaches us otherwise. Compassion and love for all and every. I make no apologies, however, for writing of the unborn again because this is one of the most intense and significant challenges the world faces. Not only this, it is also the area where people who routinely consider themselves to be progressive and sympathetic suddenly become harsh, hostile and completely lacking in empathy for one of the most numerous and persecuted victim groups on the planet.

As the last century came to its sorry close we discovered that the website for the United States government's National Institutes of Health is advertising aborted baby parts for research purposes. I wrote about it. After an introduction to the issue the column ran thus:

The commercial, worth quoting at some length, states the following.

Human embryonic and fetal tissues are available from the Central Laboratory for Human Embryology at the University of Washington. The laboratory, which is supported by the National Institutes of Health, can supply tissue from normal or abnormal embryos and fetuses of desired gestational ages between 40 days and term. Specimens are obtained within minutes of passage and tissues are aseptically identified, staged, and immediately processed according to the requirements of individual investigators.

Presently, processing methods include immediate fixation, snap fixation, snap freezing in liquid nitrogen and placement in balanced salt solutions or media designated and/or supplied by investigators. Specimens are shipped by overnight express, arriving the day following procurement.

The advert is chilling in the inhuman way it speaks of human life. "Normal" embryos mean unborn children that are perfect; "abnormal" means babies with disabilities. When the piece refers to "term" it means unborn children that could survive outside the womb, possibly as late as nine months gestation. But business being what it is, even the large babies are guaranteed to arrive far quicker than the mail.

The laboratory will also provide only what is needed for any purchaser and will kindly cut up and dissect as required. It's more lucrative that way because one aborted child can be provide a leg here, an arm there, a brain somewhere else, an internal organ in yet another location. Goodness me, this is a capitalist dream. Very few overheads and a product that is increasingly available.

Grotesque as all this sounds, it is not entirely new. A company in Illinois, Opening Lines, offers $999 for brains eight weeks old or less, $400 for an intact embryo eight weeks or less, $600 for an unborn child more than eight weeks old and $550 for gonads. All prices, of course, in US currency.

The outfit publishes a brochure for abortion facilities in which it states that now "you can turn your patients' decision into something wonderful." The document goes on to say,

> We know your patient's decision to have an abortion
> was carefully considered and we also know it was a
> very difficult one to make ... we can train your staff
> to harvest and process fetal tissue. Based on your
> volume we will reimburse part or all of your employ-
> ee's salary, thereby reducing your overhead.

Or to put it another way, there's a lot of money to be made here. Hey, nothing new. Henry Morgentaler has become a wealthy man through his work in the abortion industry. But the good doctor is a pauper compared to some of his comrades south of the border.

Although it is technically illegal to sell body parts in the United States, those involved get around the law by "donating" organs and then receiving what is known as a site fee. So abortion is, as we have long known, a big business, yet we are still thought foolish enough to believe that it is all about choice. Desperate women who go to aborturaries are told that this might not be the right thing and that they should consider all the possibilities. Sure, and I've got a full head of hair.

One of the most poignant, and sickening, ironies of all this is that much of the macabre crop is used for research into HIV/AIDS. While everything human must be done to find a cure for this plague, it is hard to deny that the majority of sufferers in North America contracted the disease through perverse sex. Ninety-five percent of the world's AIDS population is in the developing world and lack even basic health care. Nobody cared very much about these men and women before AIDS was brought to North America and, frankly, nobody cares very much now. They're poor and they're black and don't know Elizabeth Taylor or Barbara Streisand.

If experimentation must take place it should take place on animals. But I forgot. That would mean hurting little kittens and puppies and it just wouldn't be right. After all, we're human beings and cruelty is unacceptable.

Rose

 Let us consider Rose, a young, attractive woman and very much in love with the man she had recently married. Village life had never been easy in their part of Poland, but a combination of hard work and God's grace kept them in one piece. The crops grew, the sun shone and she had just found out that she was pregnant.

She was part of a Jewish family that had arrived almost five hundred years earlier, and had known darkness and light. But by 1890 the Russians were in control and there was much state-sanctioned anti-semitism. Mobs of drunken men would raid, rape and murder.

It was, said the patriarch of the clan, time to move on. So with tears in their eyes for the land and for the many local people who had been their friends they packed up what little they owned and by cart and foot moved westwards.

The journey was hard at first, but soon became agony. As borders were crossed, villages entered and passed, the group of refugees sometimes met charity, sometimes indifference but too often downright hostility. They were stoned in one place. But on they went, knowing that there was no other direction in which to travel.

Rose was showing by now, and told the assembled cousins, aunts, uncles and community that she was expecting a baby. Her husband gripped her hand as she shared the good news. Of course they were pleased, they wanted her to know that. But she had to realize that the trip was far from over, and that it would be almost impossible for her in a few weeks.

One man stepped forward to have his say. He had served in the Russian army for half his life after being kidnapped from his home when a teenager. He still had the ring that was put through his ear inscribed with the words, "Property of the Tsar." He had seen much. "They will not let you on boats and trains if they see you're with child," he said. "You'll lose the baby anyway. Better to lose it now and save yourself."

She felt her head swim. She had heard about these things going on but had never heard them suggested. He wanted her to kill her baby, to get rid of it, to have an abortion. No, she said. No, no, no. She would not do such a thing, never. And then she cried.

A very old woman put her arms around Rose and whispered in Yiddish. "Don't do what they say, but do what you know to be right." But how do I know what is right, she said. "Listen to your conscience, which is made and formed by God."

She was not very religious, not compared to some, but the words left an impression. She ran to her husband, who simply held her and said only that it was their child, but that she had to carry it and that it was her life that was at risk on the journey.

Onwards they went. The snow and the cold stopped, the land became less bold, the people more open. The baby grew bigger. Finally, after what seemed like an endless story of horror, they reached a port, larger than anything she had ever seen. She could barely walk now, and she had terrible pains in her stomach. She thought the baby might be dead.

The former soldier had been right in most of his warnings, and in predicting that they would be denied passage on a ship because of her state. The captain of the ancient steamer said he couldn't take her. She pleaded, but he understood not a word. Then she felt a cramp, so bad that she bent over. The hardened, rough old sailor rushed to help her. As he did so he looked into her eyes. "All right," he shouted, "just this once. Go on, climb aboard before I change my mind."

They boarded, and arrived safely in London, England the next day. Where they settled. And where Rose, my great grandmother, gave birth to my grandmother, who gave birth to my father. Thank you grandma. For life.

I met Rose, and liked her very much. She was very old, I was very young. She was what we might call a wise woman, full of a natural learning and a great, uncluttered wisdom. We didn't discuss politics very often, but I often wonder today what she would think of the world and its players. What, indeed, she would think of the arguments around and about life? She would, I know, speak up for the vulnerable. And there are few as vulnerable as the unborn.

Rose was a fighter for the underdog, and would have realized that what should be the safest haven of all, the womb, has become a war zone, a place of danger. She would have read the scientific evidence for the sanctity of life before birth, and also appreciated the moral and Biblical arguments against taking the life of a child at any and every stage of its development.

But she would also, I think, have realized that life contained many aspects, and danger had many forms. She would have been surprised, perhaps amazed, at those people who offer unconditional love for the unborn but appear to have a severely conditional affection for the born.

It comes down to this. We have to be genuinely pro-life rather than anti-abortion. Indeed it is one of the factors that have tended to marginalize the pro-life movement. We look foolish, incomplete, even hypocritical, when we are passionate about the rights of a child in the womb but say nothing about the mass bombing of a civilian population, the murderous exploitation of an undeveloped nation or the fortunes spent on nuclear arsenals whilst legions of mothers watch their babies die of starvation before their eyes.

Nor is it merely that too many pro-lifers are quiet on these issues. Some appear to assume that to even discuss them is a digression, or that if someone does they are extreme, left-wing and not committed to the cause. Sad. Because the struggle has nothing to do with how righteous we feel, but how effective we can be in spreading the truth of life. Life being the gift of God, who cares as much for the man hiding in the bomb shelter as He does for the tiny baby in the womb.

On Holidays

I wrote the following articles in a secular chain of newspapers with a mass readership, in which I contribute a weekly column. Christians often ask if I am allowed to do such things, assuming that if I write of my faith or speak out as a believer I will lose my job or worse. This is just not so. There are of course people in media who are fearful or hateful of Christians, but then there are Christians who are fearful, even hateful, of the secular world.

I have always found that it is the manner of presentation that shapes the response, at least with most editors, peers, readers. To be hindered by the small minority of extremists would be to let them win. There is also the issue of balance. If every column I wrote was explicitly about Jesus and my faith in Him my employers might question my purview. "Is there not more to write about?" And they'd be right.

But Christ is to be found in every issue, every cause and every debate, whether we mention Him by name or not. At

Easter and Christmas, however, and frankly on every other occasion possible and plausible, I write about my saviour. For His sake. But most of all for the sake of those who haven't yet heard about Him.

Easter

First He is interrogated, abused, threatened, both by the imperialist thugs who have raped His country and by the collaborators who have allowed the invaders to have their way. Then a group of soldiers throw Him to the ground, beat Him and spit in His face. They make fun of Him, push Him around, punch and shove Him. But the sport is just beginning.

He is tied to a post and whipped with a weapon so cruel that it often causes death. It's a multi-stringed whip, each strap weighted with lead balls that rip and tear lumps of flesh off the body. So bad are these thrashings that they expose the bowels and organs of the victim. If death doesn't occur at the time it usually takes place days later when infection sets in.

As part of the mockery one of the soldiers suggests that they make Him look like a king. After all, he shouts, He claimed to be a king. They all laugh loudly, enjoying what all bullies enjoy. A pretend crown is made, composed of the razor-sharp thorns that grow so readily in the area. They are around four inches long and so dangerous that the locals use them like knives.

The clumsy headpiece, consisting of dozens of thorns, resembles an upturned bowl. It is placed on top of His head and then pushed, hard, down onto and into His scalp. It lacerates and slices the skin, causing even more pain and loss of blood.

A crossbeam weighing more than a hundred pounds is slung across His shoulders and He is shoved into the public streets, forced to carry the weight to His place of execution. Already faint from agony and exhaustion He drops to the ground, where He is shouted at and kicked. People He considered friends and brothers turn away and hide. Old enemies laugh at the state He is in.

More soldiers scream at Him to stop. They push Him down to the ground and step over Him like He was dirt beneath their feet. Three of them hold Him down while another produces a set of thick, rusting nails six inches long, and a large, heavy mallet. The first nail is hammered into His wrist. The initial blow of the mallet pounds on the head of the nail, splitting flesh and ligament, splattering blood over His body and over the sandals and tunics of the guards.

Another nail, into the other wrist. And then the area around the ankles. Sometimes it takes several blows, sometimes the skin and muscle simply cave in, so weak have they become. The world spins, the people shout, the overwhelming pain washes with the confusion and the fear into an ocean of horror.

This is a form of judicial murder so evil that even the ruling authorities will abolish it soon afterwards as being too cruel. He has been treated with the very worst kind as well. Often wrongdoers are tied to the cross and left to die of thirst and exposure. But not Him. Every sinew of His body screams out for relief. So alone, so despised, so perfectly and utterly good.

Death will come when there is no strength left to lift the chest and breathe. It is excruciating to breathe at all because it puts pressure on the wounds, but nothing can extinguish the lust for life. Finally, though, the muscles give way, the blanket of numbness smothers all else and it stops. It stops.

A soldier pushes his spear into His side and a mixture of blood and water gushes forth. The sure sign of death. They take Him down. But it is still not enough. Guard His body and tomb, the collaborators demand. So they do.

Then the world begins again. First a few, then more, then hundreds see Him alive. They feel His wounds, eat with Him, laugh with Him, weep with Him. So sure are they of His resurrection and truth that they themselves are prepared to face deaths as bad as His. They abandon selves so as to gain everything.

Today? He is still abused, beaten, mocked and spat upon. Crazed zealots run into His churches and try to destroy the sacred; the state television system runs a show depicting a woman feeding His body and blood to a dog. It hurts, very much indeed. But in the final analysis it does not matter. Because He died, because He rose, because He is risen. For you and for me.

Christmas

 Happy Holidays from all the businesses, corporations, politicians, banks, schools, government departments and individuals who are too cowardly to risk annoying someone.

A very Happy Holidays from all those who are prepared to abandon their history, identity and faith in the name of contemporary banality and the aching blandness of the politically correct lexicon.

The obsessive fear on the part of those who refuse to say Merry Christmas seems to be that if they refer to the season of love, forgiveness and salvation they will slightly offend other people. Causing offence. The great sin of our time. And the great lie. In fact, by trying not to offend anyone, people who say Happy Holidays offend almost everyone who has any common sense. Most people have thicker skins, larger brains and a more stable grasp of the righteousness of majority will than secular liberals would have us believe.

This is Christmas because, quite simply, it is Christmas. The only reason the season exists is that our society, founded as it was upon the principles of Christianity, injected the diamond-bright time of charity and hope into our year. The great mythical dragon of offence is apparently easily provoked, however, so we have to be extremely careful.

But if we are going to be truly atheistic about all this we should at least be consistent. Happy Holidays still drips with religiosity. Holiday is the shortened version of Holy Day. It must go. I suggest Jolly Day of Recreation, Merry Time Off or even Happy Hangover. Otherwise, we might offend someone.

Then there is the calendar we observe. Goodbye to all that. The calendar we use was introduced by Pope Gregory XIII in 1582 as a correction of the one adopted by Julius Caesar. It might be ingenious and accurate, but that is hardly the point. Old Gregory was a Roman Catholic, a Pope and a European. Thus, by origin the calendar is, obviously, deeply offensive.

If you live in any city or town that is named after a saint—well, time to move or to change the name of your dwelling place. We really cannot allow such religious intrusions into our way of life in case someone is offended. How about Living Zone 14, Dwelling Area 24 or even State Approved Community 823B? Some of the beauty, romance and originality might be lost but this is, I think, a small price to pay for not offending anyone.

If your name is Christine or Christopher, or for that matter any name inspired by a saint, disciple, apostle or any Biblical character, get thee another. This would mean a great many new names. But such a chore must not stand in the way of progress. After all, words can offend.

The flags of the country simply have to be adapted. So

many of them contain a cross, a symbol that, according to our masters, causes millions of people to scream in disgust and outrage.

These could be replaced by large red banners emblazoned with pictures of terribly fashionable secular politicians or a campaigner for the rights of atheists.

There is hardly any point in my referring to "thou shall not kill," "love thy neighbor" or "turn the other cheek" being unacceptable. They are drenched in religion and hugely offensive. The list goes on.

What this is all really about is fixing something that is not and never has been broken. When I see the millions of signatures affixed to the petitions calling for an end to Christmas I might think again. When I see the tears of thousands of children driven to despair because someone wished them a Merry Christmas I will reconsider.

Until then I will remain convinced the people trying to expunge Christmas from our lives are the same people who wish to dismantle all that is good, all that is healthy and all this is right with this country and this culture.

A very merry and completely unapologetic Christmas to all of you. From a man named after an overly aggressive male who stabbed a poor, innocent fallen angel named Lucifer and has thus provoked and, yes, offended, the devil community ever since.

If only he had been more sensitive.

Rejoice

Let us talk turkey, if you will excuse the pun. Tomorrow is the anniversary of the birth of Jesus Christ. As a Christian, the day represents for me the beginning of everything. As a participant in the public discourse it raises for me a series of political and social questions. So as a Christian journalist I have one or two things to say this eve.

I will not wish anyone "Happy Holidays." This is Christmas. To pretend it is some incidental vacation is insulting to a world religion and to the intelligence of thinking people. A similar argument can be made for other religions that have a festival in December. I have enormous respect for Judaism and for the Jewish people. As such I will not dilute Hanukkah, an ancient celebration of liberation and the evidence of God, to a generic and banal phrase that stinks of political correctness.

In our obsession with inclusiveness we have, ironically, excluded almost everyone who possesses anything more than the most trivial of belief systems. Differences of faith always have and always will exist, and to pretend they do not is to deny the very importance of those beliefs in the first place, which is in itself discriminatory. When we try to meet in the middle we meet nowhere at all. Better to acknowledge our differences and to disagree with mutual respect and, vital this, with love.

The British rabbi who said recently that assimilation was a greater threat to Judaism than the Holocaust was roundly condemned. But he had a point. Religion is killed not by cruelty but by kindness. Christians best retained their Christianity when the state hated them. Compare Poland or Uganda with Holland or Canada.

Yet nor must we forget that modern North America was founded by Christian people on Christian principles. The country is now post-Christian, but its laws and virtues are solidly rooted in Christian morality.

The reason so many of the world's immigrants want to go to Canada, the U.S., Britain, Australia and Europe is precisely because those countries, founded on Christian ideals, are so accepting and pluralistic. This is not and never has been the case with, for example, the vast bulk of the Islamic world.

Unfortunately it seems that every Christmas a few parents decide to object to something like the singing of carols in their children's school. They impose their minority will because an over-sensitive teaching staff no longer knows when to tell some people to shut up.

In Buffalo just last week a crib was removed because of a handful of objections and in some public schools every indication that Christmas might be Christian is aggressively expunged. Oddly enough, there is also a trend to invite wizards and sorcerers into schools at Halloween to explain the feminist and humanist significance of witchcraft.

This year we will also all be able to work and shop on Boxing Day. And if we are allowed, it means that most of us will. It would take a brave person indeed to lose customers because he refuses to open up store on December 26. Society is tearing at the seams because families are hurting; families are hurting because they spend insufficient time together; Boxing Day was a time when families relaxed as a unit.

I applaud the capitalist work ethic but I also know that a healthy capitalist system requires a bedrock of tradition and community structure. Capitalism developed as a direct result of the Protestant Reformation and out of the admission by the great reformers that Christianity must accommodate business and commerce, and that business and commerce must accommodate Christianity.

What actually lies at the root of all this confusion is an ambivalence, even an embarrassment, about who we are. Practicing, nominal and even merely cultural Christians have for 20 years been apologizing for creating in the western world what is the most tolerant, civilized and productive society in the history of humanity. Until we stop it, until we refuse to surrender to the whims of liberal revisionism, we cannot advance.

I wish you all a very happy Christmas, I wish you prosperity, and I wish you the peace of Jesus Christ.

Brandsma

Titus Brandsma was a small, gentle, bespectacled man. He spent years working with the Dutch underground movement to smuggle Jewish people out of the Netherlands and away from the threat of the Nazi murderers. As a monk he rejected violence and so would not, could not, pick up a gun to use against the oppressors of goodness and all he held dear. But night after night, week after week, he struggled in his own way to do what had to be done.

Until he was caught. Until he was tortured, beaten, smashed and sentenced to death. As the Nazi nurse gave him a fatal injection he looked up, gave the uniformed killer his rosary beads and said "I forgive you, I'll pray for you."

Not far away, in Germany itself, a young Lutheran minister called Dietrich Bonhoeffer had returned to his homeland from abroad even though he knew the extreme danger. Precisely because, in fact, he knew of the extreme danger. He joined the German resistance and worked without pause to bring down the regime of the Hitler gang. Like his comrade across the border in Holland, he was arrested and imprisoned. Unlike his Dutch brother, he was on one occasion presented with the chance to escape. He did not take it, aware that if he had done so the Nazis would have arrested and murdered his entire family. Bonhoeffer was executed at the age of 39. He died forgiving his captors and smiling in the certainty of his future.

The reason I write of these two men is that this is Easter Week, Holy Week, the week of Good Friday and of Easter Sunday. It is the most sacred time in the Christian year and commemorates the death and resurrection of Jesus Christ, the precise reason why Brandsma, Bonhoeffer and so many others were able to live and die with such splendor. They did not "change with the times" as so many did then and so many do now, they did not become hateful and they did not surrender. They fought and they forgave. And they did so not because of liberalism or relativism or nationalism or socialism, but because they were utterly convinced that what happened on the first Easter was completely true. Oh, for a few more people who thought the same now.

Easter, however, is getting a hard time of it. The culture and the state have transformed what was the motivation for Brandsma and Bonhoeffer into a few days when we can buy and sell chocolate eggs and chase a little yellow bunny around the backyard. There has been an attempt, conscious and unconscious, to expunge Christianity and meaning out of Easter.

But without Christianity there is no Easter and without Easter there are no Christians who devote their lives to ending slavery like William Wilberforce, no heroes who give their all to do away with child labor like Lord Shaftesbury, no champions of racial equality and non-violence like Martin Luther King. The body politic, North America and the modern world would be very different without people like this, people who worked tirelessly and courageously not because of nicely packaged candy, but because of their certain knowledge of Easter and all it represents.

Indeed the very political foundations of North America are based on a European enlightenment that was Christian to the core. Of course there are abuses and of course we have made mistakes, but notions of pluralism, tolerance and human dignity do not come from thin air or from the backroom of some party conference. They did not exist in the pagan world and they do not exist today in many parts of the non-Christian world. We only need to look at the history of the vehemently anti-religious Soviet empire to realize that.

So Easter is about more than a day off and a sugar rush. It is about a Dutch monk, a German theologian and about tens of millions of people persecuted across the world for their beliefs. It is about love, forgiveness, hope and charity. It is about freedom, goodness and about a young Jewish man who died in agony in a faraway corner of an ancient empire. And about his resurrection. Believe it or don't believe it but, please, don't ignore it. You really can't. Happy Easter.

ON SEXUALITY

*H*ere are two columns about sexuality. The first deals with the issue of homosexuality and the second with mainstream sexuality, marriage and what the contemporary world considers to be romantic love. As I have tried to make clear in the first essay, we have to be extremely careful to approach these very personal issues with Christian love as well as Christian boldness. It is all too easy to choose an area where, perhaps, we are not ourselves tempted and to blast away at those who are not as fortunate. This is surely not what Christ called us to do.

Gay

The issue of homosexuality is perhaps the most difficult one about which a Christian is obliged to write. It is about real, breathing, loving, often hurting people. More than this, to oppose the various demands of Gay people is seen by many to be cruel and uncaring. They have a point. Hatred and ignorance has been behind much of the opposition to homosexuality over the years and to a certain extent still is.

We're probably all guilty, and I know that there are some things I have written in the past that I would not say now. But to refine one's attitude towards a situation does not necessarily mean that one changes one's overall stance. For me the supreme position must be no compromise on truth, no compromise on love.

A few observations. First, it is odd that people who routinely hurl abuse at anti-poverty groups, unions and social activists and who call for ever more attacks on welfare and public funding are so very liberal on issues like homosexuality. I have seen this time and time again. Journalists and commentators who make a living out of labeling people as extremists or as unrepresentative leaders of special interest groups, who champion banks and corporations, suddenly become all sensitive and sympathetic when sexuality is the issue.

It's the phenomenon of the lifestyle liberal. The campaign for supposed Gay rights is to a large extent a middle-class battle, one supported by money and the market because money and the market believe in low taxes and low morals. The neo-conservative rides again.

Protest the closing of a hospital or the shooting of a black youth by the cops and we'll call you a zealot. Ask for two men to be married and we'll cry for their pain.

Second, the bias shown by media in the reporting on Gay issues is quite extraordinary. Interesting this, in that marriage is usually mocked and marginalized. People get married all the time, sacrifice for one another, remain faithful to one another, love one another, raise children together, nurse one another. Yet newspapers, television and movies seem to promote infidelity and laugh at the stable married couple. Perhaps it's just because they're boring old heterosexuals.

Third, there are crazy people on all sides. Some of those protesting all this have shamed the cause and the man they claim they represent. They evince venom and coldness and seem to be obsessed with this particular issue. Equally there are some in the Gay community who are horribly intolerant. I can show you the death threats and know all too well of the attempts to have me fired.

But these two groups represent the polarized borders. In-between there is much room for dialogue and understanding. And dialogue and understanding there must be. Gay people live together, always will live together and, whilst we might disagree with their lifestyle, are entitled to name partners as legal and financial beneficiaries. Equally, marriage was conceived to describe only one thing: the union of a man and a woman.

A domestic partnership? A recognized civil union that does not in any way diminish or alter the unique status of marriage? I don't know exactly. I do know that currently the political and social fashion is with Gay people but that fashion has no answers. A genuine resolution please, with compassion and empathy all 'round. Shouting will solve nothing. We all need to be reminded of that.

Every time I am tempted to react too strongly I remember that I, at least, am sexually broken and there is a very good chance that you are as well. I thank God that my temptations, my flaws, are not of a homosexual nature. I can only imagine how difficult life would be if they were. There are many sins in the world and many sinners. Perhaps if the church had in the past been more egalitarian in its critiques we would be more accepted now when we speak out on issues such as homosexuality.

Which is why have to respect, but oppose, those Gay people who try to carve out a Gay Christian theology in the midst of their sexual struggle. They want a relationship with God. The shame is that they already have one, and have already been told by Him how to sharpen it. But the sharpening process is not always easy. Their arguments may be the product of pain and need, but even so we have to show them for what they really are.

The idea, for example, that King David had a homosexual relationship with Jonathan is pretty thin stuff. Anyone who understands the Hebrew Bible and the Hebrew people will know that the Scriptures simply don't say this. These men were like brothers, and the fact they had a platonic relationship is emphasized.

In the fact the Jewish people had a particular rejection of homosexuality. Many pagan cultures of the ancient world, including Greek and Roman, ignored or even encouraged homosexuality at different stages of their history. But the Jews would not tolerate it for a moment. Goodness me, logic has to be heard. If David had been a homosexual, his friendship with Jonathan would not have been recorded by those who admired him. Nor would he have been revered by those who regarded homosexuality as a terrible sin.

Another aspect of the argument is that the prohibition on homosexuality found in the Old Testament is no longer valid, because we don't observe all of the other prohibitions in, say, Leviticus or Deuteronomy. This is a basic misreading and misunderstanding of the Bible. Dietary laws do change, but moral ones do not. The New Testament shows us how Christ, Peter, Paul and the founding church moved away from some of the cosmetic rules of the old covenant but not the moral and ethical aspects of the teaching. If anything emphasized and enforced it.

Nor is homosexuality condemned only in the Old Testament but is also mentioned in the New. It is true that Jesus does not refer to it specifically, but in His words on sexual purity and His very existence as the fulfillment of prophecy His supposed silence echoes around the world to the end of time. There are many things he did refer to by name. We find no condemnation of genocide; are we to construe from this that the Messiah did not have an opinion on such a crime?

Beyond the prohibitions are the positive commands. They are splendid in that they were provided for us to enjoy the beauty of creation, of the world, of each other. With limits and boundaries. The entire creation story is based on the differences between the genders. Of course this can be difficult to accept. Faith is not always easy, but it is always correct.

What we must remember, however, is the simultaneous approach of Christ's love and the Christian's response to sin. Love, understanding and the acceptance of repentance and transformation. Poppy is a perfect example. She came to see me after a speech I gave one freezing night in a large rural church. Her first words were, "Can you be a Christian and homosexual?" We chatted for more than half-an-hour, and were both shaking with the cold. Truth be told, she was also shaking out of fear. What she did was extremely brave.

Her story was far from unusual, and saying this will immediately hurt some Gay people. She was a product of abuse. An uncle and a neighbour had molested her. Poppy's parents had been unloving. The first person to show her love and affection was another woman. I've heard such stories time and time again. Not always the case, but sufficiently frequent to present a pattern.

We spoke, we wrote, she met with a local minister. We all prayed. Six months later she gave her life to Jesus Christ. This happens. Far more often than Gay people would want us to believe, perhaps far less often than some Christians would have us believe. Because sometimes there is no change. Take Rebecca, who is now an ordained Baptist minister.

She had been a lesbian for ten years before she found herself somewhat reluctantly a believer in God and Jesus Christ. "I read through the Bible, every page and paragraph, so many times. I was looking for a way out, a loop-hole that would allow me to be a Christian and continue as a lesbian." A pause for breath and to fight back emotion.

"I couldn't change. I was attracted to women, not to men. So I realized what I had to do. I would have be celibate for the rest of my life. That was twenty years ago. It's not easy. In fact it's very, very tough. But Christ has multiplied His love for me so as to compensate. I'm not saying that I never cry about it. But after the dark comes the light. And oh what a light it is."

The debate will continue. Who knows where it will end. If there is any hatred in your heart you have no right to speak out on the subject. If there is love in your heart you have a responsibility to speak out on the subject. As followers of He who is love itself.

Valentine

I'm severely ambivalent about Valentine's Day. Of course I adore giving my wife a card and a present, and receiving the same from her. But the day also gives yet another opportunity for people to claim that they remembered love, so that they could forget for the rest of the year. Because we love everything, don't we. We love the show we just saw, love the pop group we just heard, love the flavour we just tried, love the person we just had sex with. What the hell has love got to do with it?

Love, romantic love, the love between a man and a woman must be put right. Because too many people have been trying to put it wrong. A few basics. No sex before marriage, fidelity to your partner after marriage, no divorce and a commitment to raising a family.

And what is extraordinary, what is truly extraordinary, is that many people who have just read that paragraph are incredulous, even angry. "I don't believe he could have written such a thing, I mean, is this guy for real? Why doesn't he change with the times?"

Yes I'm for real, and as for changing for the times, no. How could anyone want to change with the times when we have just exited the most murderous century in history. Would we ask a German in 1939 to change with the times?

First, the sex before marriage myth. A line as tired as a sleepwalker on a treadmill. We've all heard it. Unless you experiment with one another and find out if you're sexually compatible the marriage will never work. You might not click.

Horse feathers. Pre-marital sex became common only in the last forty years and all experts agree that its rate of occurrence multiplied enormously after the 1960s. Which, strangely enough, is precisely when divorce became so common. Far from guaranteeing that we were happy together, sex before marriage made it far more likely that marriages would fail. So much for the compatibility argument.

In fact all promiscuity achieves is a need for more promiscuity. Which is pretty much common sense. The really important factors in keeping a marriage together involve time spent outside of the bed, and these are precisely the factors that we jettisoned in the glorious rush towards so-called sexual liberation.

Actually sexual incompatibility is incredibly rare. When physical attraction and love are combined the result is sexual pleasure. Add to this the dignity of saving yourself for the person you love and joy is certain. All the arguments about the desperate need to behave like rabbits in rebellion are based not on logic but on lust. "I don't want to wait, why should I." The Me Generation.

Which brings me to the rate of sexually transmitted diseases and so-called unwanted pregnancies. They have risen every year since the universal availability of contraceptives and the advent of that great feminist pharmaceutical, the

Pill. It would all be okay now, we were told, the sexual revolution will save our souls. Not quite. As some pointed out at the time, rather than save our souls it would sink our ship.

Look for yourself. Not only in North America but in every country where contraceptives are introduced the rate of sexual diseases and abortions are multiplied. Replace love with latex and we encourage irresponsibility. You might not like to hear the truth but that does not make the truth any less truthful. And you won't hear such truth very often.

Then we have divorce. Without doubt past marriages sometimes stayed together when they should have broken up. But these were relatively few. Ignore the social revisionists who have an axe to grind, the fact is that divorce is never positive. In fact divorce equals failure. If you have divorced, you have failed.

I heard a man say just the other day that his parents' divorce was the best thing that happened to him because mum and dad argued so much. No, no, no. The best thing that could have happened to you would have been if your parents had stopped arguing! Because divorce hurts kids and even sociological liberals now admit that single-parent families are never ideal.

We're not animals, we're not beyond self-control, there is glory in commitment, love involves sacrifice. And I'm tired of the sordid thinking they're the clever ones. Because they're not.

ON PARENTING

I have written about spanking and corporal punishment several times. Not because I have any particular interest in the subject, but because others certainly have. In that they want to make it illegal. I oppose this. On the other hand I have severe problems with those Christians who seem to think that unless you support spanking and spank your children you are in danger of losing your salvation. Call me a rash son of a gun if you like, but I think I'll take my chances.

Scripture is not as clear as some people like to think on this issue. Whether it calls for parents to spank their children is very much an issue of debate. What we can be certain of is that it does not forbid parents to spank their children. God demands love, compassion and empathy. But he also requires responsibility and the appropriate use of authority. In other words, give your kids a tap on the behind if you really think it fit. But don't feel that you have to do so. And if you do spank, make it rare and extremely moderate.

Most of all, don't make it a major issue. We followers of Jesus tend to fall into the traps set by our critics when they obsess about various issues. Instead of responding with balance, we tend to rush headlong into the fight. Corporal punishment is one very small subject. Not to be ignored, but not to become dominant.

I have also included a column on parenting in general, and the way in which children and parents are sometimes caricatured by some in the media.

Spanking

 My personal view is that spanking doesn't achieve very much. The occasional pat on the bum with an open hand might be necessary, or a spank on a child's hand or the top of a leg. There is a very limited age window when this might be helpful, and more often than not there are other ways to achieve the task. But it doesn't really matter. I say again, it doesn't really matter.

The great irony of all this is that child abuse has probably never been greater. And there has never been as little corporal punishment of children. By abuse I mean, for example, the indifference shown by so many parents, the lack of love. The absence of proper parenting with boundaries, discipline and the sacrifice of time.

Little girls dressed up as Madonna or as miniature hookers, boys as pimps and pushers. Give the ten-year-old the cell phone, free access to the internet and a television in their bedroom. Presents from mum and dad instead of presence of mum and dad. Let them do what they want to do when they want to do it. Make them sexual when they should be silly, let them be materialistic when they should be merry, foul-mouthed when they should be fancy-free.

I fully respect a person's right never to spank their children. Odd, then, that the zealots amongst the non-spankers have no respect for the parenting approach of other people. We should also scratch the surface of what these extremists really believe. Not only is any form of physical punishment seen as being unacceptable but also the raising of a parental voice towards a child and the sending of a child to their bedroom.

"To shout or be loud to a young person is tantamount to abuse," explained one young woman to me. "I mean, would you do this to your wife? Would you strike your wife as well if she had done something wrong?"

The answer is no. But nor would I demand that she did her homework when she wanted to go to the park to play soccer, nor would I say that she could not have any more candy and nor would I demand that she go to school, respect her elders and tidy her room. If I did, well she might end up giving me a clip 'round the ear. Oh gosh, I've made light of the most serious issue in the history of the world!

It's interesting that the teachers' unions, not always the bastions of conservative thought, are solidly behind the right to use mild force when children are involved. The reason? Obvious. They are on the front line and grasp the reality of the situation.

The same young woman who told me of the repugnance of a parent raising a voice to a child also gave me a lecture about, "the laziness of parents who spank or shout instead of listening to some of the latest sociological evidence. Use time-outs, redirection programmes, affirmative support action." Interesting. Time-outs and affection—now why didn't any of the rest of us think of that?

Then we have the consequences of the repeal of the law that allows mild spanking of a child. The zealots deny it, but if the law is changed it will be illegal to use any kind of force against a child. In other words a hysterical child in a store cannot be put over a shoulder and taken home. If a complaint is made, the parent would be visited by a social worker and even lose custody. If you doubt me, look at the history of Sweden since it altered its laws.

Abuse is always wrong, the habitual use of corporal punishment is wrong, inflicting pain on a child is wrong. But some people confuse proper childraising with their own permissive self-indulgence. Do as you wish, but don't impose fashionable nonsense on the rest of us. It would be terribly abusive.

Gavin

Gavin was having a bad day. A very bad day indeed. And when 5-year-old boys have bad days everybody gets to know about it. He began to kick the cat. His father told him to stop it. Gavin refused, and gave the creature another few kicks. At which point Joe Cleary did what many parents might do. He gave his son a spanking. End of story.

But no. The spanking on the bum left a very slight mark and this was noticed by a teacher at Gavin's swimming lesson. The teacher reported it to her supervisor, who in turn reported it to the local Children's Aid Society.

The first thing that happened was a telephone call from a young social worker to Joe's wife, Perry, the mother of their six children. The social worker wanted clarification of the incident and requested an interview with little Gavin. "I'll have to speak to my husband first," said the heavily pregnant Perry. The social worker was incredulous, even annoyed. Why on earth did she have to speak to her husband?

"Because" replied Perry, "he is my husband, because he is Gavin's father and because he is the head of the house."

There is an expression concerning a bull and a red rag that comes to mind. The social worker seemed extremely angry now, almost beyond reason.

It was a month later when the police came to arrest Joe Cleary. They came to where he worked, handcuffed him in front of his workmates and employers and took him away like some rapist or murderer. He was charged with assault and was told by the police that he really should make a statement before his lawyer arrived because if he didn't it would look bad in court. Joe had nothing at all to hide and so he made a statement.

This good, honest, hard-working man was now incarcerated for two days in a holding cell and then in the town jail, where prisoners are kept for up to two years. He had to fend off sexual advances from other men, had to watch out for the men around him charged with unspeakable crimes of violence and sadism.

After a brief court appearance the court asked for $1000 bail. His wife managed to get the money and offered it to the court. She was turned down, because of a statement she had made to the 22-year-old social worker on the phone. She had referred to her husband as being "the head of the house" and this was to be used in court by the prosecution, the accusation being that the couple had a "slave-master" relationship.

So the money had to be found elsewhere, and this wasn't easy for a large family who put their children first and had limited personal savings. But they managed. The bail conditions initially prevented Joe from having any contact with minors, effectively stopping him from seeing his family. Perry, now with a 10-day-old baby in her arms, protested so loudly that eventually her husband was allowed to return home.

The couple had to go to court a further seven times, with the crown demanding continuances and further investigations. "It was almost as if they were trying to punish us," say the Clearys. The couple's legal bills eventually totaled $10,000 but their lawyers were so outraged by what was going on that they halved the cost.

Finally the judge dismissed the charges, but the whole family was and is still in shock and Joe is hardly confident of promotion at work after he was seen being arrested and his bosses read about his court appearances. If it hadn't been for the strength of his union Joe Cleary may well have been fired.

As for young Gavin, none of the people behind this persecution seemed to care very much about him one way or the other. It seemed to be his parents they were after. He is, by the way, an extraordinarily happy and content little boy. The only thing that worries him these days is the idea of social workers and policemen coming to take his daddy away.

His parents are more concerned about those people who want to remove the right of mothers and fathers to chastise their children. Such zealots quote the United Nations Charter forbidding spanking, a document that also says that if little Johnny or Jenny run to their room and slam their door shut no parent has the right to enter. It would be an "infringement" on the child's personal space and could even be "emotional abuse."

Do look behind the gentle façade of the so-called children's rights activists and do question their agenda. If you have any doubts, just have a talk with Joe and Perry Cleary. If you can still find them, because they are so upset and disillusioned that they are considering leaving their home and moving far, far away.

Children

There have been dozens of reports in the past ten years telling us what we surely already knew. Namely that the rate of illiteracy amongst school children is high and getting higher. As someone who grew up in a working-class home in east London in Britain, I have little time for those people who excuse children everything if they're not middle-class. It's an insult to my heritage and upbringing. Yet nor will I play the game of looking back with painfully nostalgic glasses and pretending that all was fine in the past. I will, I hope, state a few truths and not care about offending ideologies of all stripes.

In 2000 another report about education was published and I decided to make my views known.

Last week's report about the startling lack of literacy amongst high school students should really come as no surprise to anyone. Nor should the fact that the usual suspects are using this revealed failure as a clumsy stick with which to strike teachers. The mantra is simple and predictable.

Kids are not making the grade, thus teachers are to blame. A conclusion so crass that anyone making it should question their own educational level.

I have said this before and I'll say it again. Of course there are some lazy, cynical and incompetent teachers. But I cannot think of a single employment group more sincere, dedicated and professional than the men and women who teach our children.

So it is certainly not teachers who are to blame for our learning crisis. In some ways it is almost everyone other than teachers.

Parents. Let children watch as much television as they want to and then complain that you can't be with them twenty-four hours a day and so can't always know what they're watching. Give them cell phones and Game Boys, let them hang out with their friends in the mall all the time but make the expected gestures about the evils of materialism.

Don't whatever you do ever say no to a demand and think it cute when your child answers back or uses foul language. Don't make them do homework if they don't feel like it, never know who they're seeing or what they're reading and say nothing when they dress like a pimp and pretend to be a gangster. And make despairing comments about the summer break and how you can't wait to pack them back to school.

Educational theorists and bureaucrats. Assume mediocrity. Be relevant. Little Johnny and Susan won't be able to cope with an esoteric novel, logical construction or ancient history so don't even try. Be relevant. Give them what they're used to. In fact make school as much an extension of home, television and movies as you can. Be relevant.

Elitism is a filthy word and Shakespeare is even dirtier. There is probably more creativity and meaning in a discussion of wrestling than a debate on Macbeth.

Oh, and be relevant. Even if relevance is what you learnt twenty years ago while you were listening to Fleetwood Mac and bringing the revolution to your suburb by smoking joints and calling your mum a reactionary. You certainly know far more about education than anyone who has ever lived before you.

Politicians. Poor kids can't read and they're all hungry because poor people don't care about their families and single mothers are too busy crying to hold their children close and listen to them, love them, laugh with them. Blame the other political party when it's in power and then do nothing to change the system in any meaningful way when you're in government.

Movie and television show makers. Produce anti-intellectual, amoral sound-bite sugar and then host "important" programmes about why and how our children can't read and write. Create an icon of indifference, absurd levels of entitlement, self-adoration and violence. But make sure that a sacred level of tolerance of all forms of sexual behaviour, except fidelity, is implicit in your product.

Right-wingers. Constantly remind people that it all went wrong when The Lord's Prayer and the strap were taken out of the schools. Blame teachers and socialism. And cheer for a free market that obliges your kids to buy expensive new clothes if they want to fit in with their friends, and a neo-conservatism that takes money out of public education and questions any university course than doesn't result in a job in trade or industry.

Left-wingers. Never, ever criticize a teacher or a union and say it all went wrong when, well, say it never really went wrong actually. It's just that we don't throw enough money at the system and it has nothing to do with standards, discipline and the decline of the traditional family. Know that children used to be beaten into a dumb submission every day of their sorry school lives and that language is merely what you feel it to be.

Children? I sincerely wonder if anyone is really listening and understanding. If so, they might be surprised at what they hear.

ON CHRISTIANS

There are three short biographies here. One of the men written about was a friend of mine. The other two I did not know. At least we didn't actually meet in the flesh. I regard them, however, as very close friends in that their lives and writings influenced and influence me now, far more than the example and work of so many people still living. We need to praise and honour Christian heroes far more than we do at the moment. Not only because they are inspirations and models, but also to remind ourselves that we are not alone, and never will be.

Tolkien

The question is asked almost every time I speak in churches and sell my books. Friendly visitors look at my works on the table and notice my biography of the author of *The Lord of the Rings*. "Oh, Tolkien," they say. "Tell me, was he a Christian?" Sometimes people are merely curious. But on other occasions it's about the cloud of insecurity lowering upon our house. In other words, if this guy isn't a believer I'm not coming near him. It's bad enough that he writes about wizards and magic. That he's going to hell too. Forget it.

In fact Tolkien was a Christian, a devoted member of the Roman Catholic Church. Which in itself will cause problems for some. But more to the point is the fact that whilst it is important to know about Tolkien's faith or lack of it, we really have to stop running away from non-Christian literature. Not only this, we have to be extremely careful about running towards Christian literature. The classics are, as the word suggests, solid and noble. But much of contemporary Christian writing is, forgive me, thin, clichéd and anti-intellectual.

Our vocation is not to run from the culture, but to change it. God has never taught us to retreat in fear but to advance with courage. It was certainly something that Tolkien did in abundance. Both during his lifetime and since his death he didn't really fit the bill. Novelists are supposed to wear their angst on their finely tailored sleeves, to be whirling dervishes of deconstruction, discontent, deviance and the divine right of protest. Yet the author of *The Hobbit* and *The Lord of the Rings* was quintessentially comfortable; in his life as well as in his tweeds.

When various bookstores, newspapers, magazines and literary societies compiled their lists of all-time greats at the end of last year, however, Tolkien won the contests over and over again. First it was a chain of stores, polling more than 25,000 people. Dickens, Tolstoy and Jane Austen did well, but the bloke with the pipe and friends in dwarfish places came out top.

This annoyed the chattering classes no end, so the highly prestigious Folio Society asked its 50,000 members. Connoisseurs of fine literature, these good men and women were certain to make a different choice. They didn't.

The question was then taken to other countries, other languages, and changed into "Best Book of the Century," "Best Author of the Century" and even "Greatest Writer of the Millennium." Like it or not, Tolkien beat Joyce, Proust and Balzac. Prompting one British critic to say that this was why universal literacy and a publicly funded library system were not so desirable. He was joking. Just.

Because nothing is so unpopular with our elites as, yes, popularity. And Tolkien is as popular as they come. In the summer of 2000 the short trailer of The Lord of the Rings movie was put on the film company's official website, part of an early publicity blitz for the release of the first of the three productions at the end of this year.

On the first day the trailor was available there were 1.5 million downloads. Twice the number for the previous record, held by Star Wars: The Phantom Menace. Informed opinion believes that *The Lord of the Rings* could be the most commercially successful movie ever made.

Why? Or, in the words of those who hate the Oxford University professor with his tales of wizards, elves, battles and mystery, why the hell does this awful man and his awful readers do so well?

The support for Tolkien is fascinating not only because of its size but because of its diversity. Devotees of science fiction, fans of dungeons and dragons, traditional Roman Catholics, zealots on the fringes of the political far right, dabblers in the occult, old hippies and, now, the new wave of people opposed to globalization and free trade.

The reason for the unholy alliance is really the nature of the man himself. He was a conservative Catholic, never happy with the reforms of the Second Vatican Council and somewhat sympathetic to the aspirations of Franco and his gang during the Spanish Civil War. This needs context. There were many British and North American Catholics who, whilst totally opposed to Hitler and Nazism, were shocked by the slaughter of priests and nuns by the Republicans in Spain and grudgingly preferred the Generalissimo to a left increasingly dominated by Stalinism and the Kremlin's thugs.

Yet Tolkien was an anti-Nazi before it was altogether respectable, and indeed when many on the political left were still ambivalent. Shortly before the Second World War a German publisher wrote to him and inquired about buying the rights to his works. They asked if he was an Aryan. He replied that the word made no linguistic or ethnic sense. But, he added, if they were in fact asking him if he had any Jewish blood he regretted that this was not the case, although he would like to have some connection with such a gifted people. He finished by telling the letter writer that he would never be allowed to publish him and that the Nazis were destroying German culture and the beauty of the northern spirit.

Tolkien's religious conservatism simply did not transfer into political reaction. Indeed it seldom does. He viewed the industrialization of his beloved Warwickshire, that country in the middle of England that inspired the characters and locations in *The Lord of the Rings*, with unrestrained horror. The working people of his youth had, he thought, a certain autonomy, a special dignity. That had been expunged with the advance of the factory, the collective, the multinational.

As for globalisation, Tolkien believed in the small community. He once said that Belgium was the perfect size for a country. Large enough to be distinct, small enough to feel like an extended family. The idea of universal free trade and a one world corporate government terrified him.

His fame and success was in essence an American phenomenon, or at least it began in the United States. Before American university students took up Tolkien's cause he had been successful on a much smaller scale. World famous in Oxford, so to speak. The new radicalism of the 1960s looked to a most surprising hero. Tolkien's books sold in quite staggering numbers and graffiti began to appear on college walls. Beneath slogans demanding withdrawal from Vietnam would be written, "Frodo Rules" and "Bilbo for President."

No surprise then that the man should be read again now by the pierced ranks determined to bring down Starbucks, Nike and international capitalism.

Science fiction and dungeons and dragons? The appeal is obvious. The issue here is that Tolkien initiated the whole thing. But whereas his emulators fill their books with babes in red leather leotards and muscular chaps in jerkins, Tolkien gave them character and depth and, yes, fundamentally Christian notions of value, virtue and truth.

So the fan base is a delicious mingling of types who would not normally give each other the time of day. The movie, their movie, will annoy as well as delight. There is none so fanatical as a Tolkien fan. By Gandalf's beard they better get, well, better get Gandalf's beard right. And as Tolkien's triumph is largely within the individual imagination, any interpretation will inevitably displease some. But that is the delight of the man and his work. Tolkien gave us the magnificent playing field, we play the game.

Lewis

 He liked to be called Jack. Plain Jack. It suited his character, or so he thought. Certainly those who knew him said that he looked like an ordinary high-street butcher. Until he spoke and until he wrote. Oh, and how he wrote. *Mere Christianity, The Screwtape Letters, Surprised by Joy* and *The Lion, The Witch and The Wardrobe* among so many others. C.S. Lewis, Clive Staples, one of the finest popular communicators of the Christian message and the Christian life.

Lewis was born in November 1898 in Belfast, Northern Ireland. As such this is his centenary and, commercialism being what it is, we are in the middle of a thunder-storm of books and videos. But it is a sweet rain and it is a joy to be made wet. Lewis would have laughed at such antics, always considering himself to be an ordinary teacher and an ordinary Christian.

In fact he was a most extraordinary teacher. A lecturer at both Oxford and Cambridge University, he was considered one of the finest minds of his generation by fellow professors. His *English Literature in the Sixteenth Century*

Excluding Drama and "The Allegory of Love" are still considered to be academic masterpieces. But it is Lewis the Christian who changed the world. His genius was the ability to convey highly complicated and complex ideas in a straightforward and understandable manner. Like some grand knight of common sense he charged through the ranks of cluttered thinking, double-talk and atheism, seldom taking any prisoners.

"There are two equal and opposite errors into which our race can fall about the devil" he wrote. "One is to disbelieve in their existence. The other is to believe, and to feel an excessive and unhealthy interest in them. They themselves are equally pleased by both errors, and hail a materialist or a magician with the same delight."

Of the increasingly common statement that Jesus might have been a great moral teacher but was not the son of God Lewis pointed out that this contradicted Christ's own claims:

A man who was merely a man and said the sort of things Jesus said would not be a great moral teacher. He would either be a lunatic—on the level with the man who says he is a poached egg—or else he would be the Devil of Hell. You can shut Him up for a fool, you can spit at Him and kill Him as a demon; or you can fall at His feet and call Him Lord and God. But let us not come with any patronizing nonsense about His being a great human teacher. He has not left that open to us. He did not intend to.

Lewis declared himself a Christian in 1929, "perhaps the most dejected and reluctant convert in all England." It was as though he had tried to avoid the inevitable, considering every argument against Christianity, forcing himself to take on all of the objections his fertile mind could produce. Each one he overcame. By the time his intellect was well and truly won over his emotional being simply fell into place.

From this point on everything he wrote was informed and enlivened by his Christianity. But Lewis was too subtle and too clever to knock people over the head with his faith. He knew that talking was far more effective than shouting. In 1950 *The Lion, The Witch and The Wardrobe* was published, the first of seven books in the Narnia series. The Christian metaphors and imagery are obvious to most adults but to children the stories are merely delicious and unforgettable. As such they have sown the seeds of belief in innumerable young minds. Certainly in mine. When as a little boy I read of a great lion king called Aslan giving his life for a bad child, of his coming to life again, of his defeating an evil queen, of a magical world that we all could enter, I could only weep with excitement. Thirty years later I weep with gratitude.

In 1952 Lewis's *Mere Christianity* appeared. The title reflected the author's attempt to remove Christianity away from those who would adapt it, alter it, dilute it, change what is pure and pristine into something that is confused and confusing. Again, he did not pepper his prose with quotes from the Scriptures because he knew that this would have a limited effect on the majority of his readers. It is seldom advisable to use Biblical statements to argue with people who do not believe in the Bible. What he did do was to show that a belief in God was logical and that from this belief an acceptance of Jesus Christ was unavoidable. He reversed the equation offered by the secular world, that it is the thoughtless who become Christians, the thoughtful who reject it. Simply, he summed up the arguments like an angel:

There is no need to be worried by facetious people who try to make the Christian hope of Heaven ridiculous by saying they do not want to spend eternity playing harps. The answer to such people is that if they cannot understand books written for grown-ups, they should not talk about them. All the scriptural imagery (harps, crowns, gold, etc) is, of course, a merely symbolical attempt to express the inexpressible. People who take these symbols literally might as well think that when Christ told us to be like doves, He meant that we were to lay eggs.

In the 1950s Lewis met and fell in love with Joy Davidman, an American convert from Judaism. The marriage was beautiful but brief and Joy died in 1960. The movie Shadowlands chronicled some of the magnificence of the relationship but managed to expunge most of the Christianity from the story. What brought them together, what sustained them during the agony of cancer and what saved Lewis after the loss was a commitment to Jesus Christ. Just as in Lewis' day, the entertainment industry is not comfortable with such a notion.

After Joy's death Lewis wrote a short book entitled *A Grief Observed*, an exploration of his own feelings following his wife's death. "Grief still feels like fear," he said. "Up till this time I always had too little time. Now there is nothing but time. Almost pure time, empty successiveness." He told friends he could no longer remember Joy's face. Until it came to him that she was there all along, just waiting. Her face shone again in his mind and God's love and certainty overwhelmed his pain.

Though his remaining years were never as happy as those spent with Joy he wrote and lectured, becoming a famous man in Europe as well as North America. He died in 1963, on the same day as President Kennedy. Because of this his death received less coverage than it might. Something that would have pleased Jack Lewis. Yet his funeral in Oxford was well attended, with so many people grieving. But grief was quite unnecessary. Lewis had known that what was to come was far greater than what we have already known. And he was reunited with Joy. As for the lion Aslan, some say they heard him roar all day, from Oxford to the ends of the Earth.

Longford

When the Earl of Longford died in 2001 almost every adult in Britain reacted in some form or another. In North America he was less known, perhaps little known. Even so, he merited half page obituaries in some newspapers and several radio and television discussions. I write about him because Lord Longford, or Frank Pakenham, or just Frank, was my Godfather.

He was 95-years-old and had led a wonderful life. So this is not the time for regrets, but for memories and statements. One being that Frank was one of those rare figures who defied political boundaries and labels.

He was a moral conservative who led crusades against pornography, declining morals and abortion. But also a social radical who called for the release from prison of some of the country's most hated convicts, who opposed the death penalty and who insisted on raising his voice in favour of the marignalized and powerless.

He was a child of privilege, from an ancient family of Anglo-Irish aristocrats. Although raised a Tory and a Protestant, he embraced socialism and Roman Catholicism and served in several Labour governments. He once told me that he had known every Prime Minister since 1930 on first-name terms. He was also a good friend of Presidents Kennedy and Nixon.

He was regarded as an eccentric. Extremely tall and slim, with tufts of hair at the side of his head and a most extraordinary ability to look untidy, he would stand up in the British Parliament and ignore the jeers of political allies and foes alike.

Why the jeers? For one because Frank championed Myra Hindley. This woman was one of the Moors Murderers, a couple who kidnapped several children and then tortured them to death. They tape-recorded the screams of their victims. Hardened policemen broke down in the courtroom.

Frank decided that Hindley had been cajoled by her lover into these devilish crimes and that after decades in prison she should be released. The British public, and successive governments, guaranteed that this would never happen.

For claiming that even the vilest of criminal may be capable of change, and may have been part victim herself, Frank Longford was vilified in the media and even physically attacked. Far from silencing him, however, the vitriol seemed to make him stronger.

Similarly with his campaign against pornography, he was mocked as "Lord Porn" and editorials and cartoonists had endless fun with his supposed enjoyment of or obsession with the stuff. In fact he was a married man with eight children and a very healthy sex life. He simply thought that depicting men and, particularly, women, as pieces of meat for the titillation of the needy and the profit of the unscrupulous was damnable.

He led a government commission on pornography and as such had to watch hours and hours of material. I once asked him if it had any effect. "Yes," he said, giving one of his ironic smiles. "It always made me rather bored, sorry and tired. But I had to admire the stamina of those young people."

He also called for a greater civility in society, for more balance in the media and for a more equal distribution of wealth. He helped establish clubs and centres for very tough inner city kids. There was something abundantly charming about seeing Frank, in crumpled suit and old school tie, chatting with steel-hard young men about their former lives as soccer hooligans. He never patronized, always listened.

Frank was at the forefront of the anti-racist movement, as well as the pro-life community. Important this. For him a belief in the sanctity of life meant all humanity, at every stage of development.

"I cannot oppose abortion unless I can be there helping that poor, single, pregnant woman find a home and a job and support," he said once, over one of our long lunches. "Otherwise I'd be a hypocrite. Can't be that. Just can't be that."

He was active and alert until the final days, even though people often thought him so old as to be out of touch. Not true. He was also proud of his friends, and showed me such pride on more than one occasion. He was a Christian gentleman, in every sense of the phrase. I miss him. So does everyone who knew and understood him.

ON EUGENICS

The following is an essay about HG Wells, about whom I wrote a large biography some years ago. I can't pretend that the book was enjoyable for me. Wells is important is many ways; and arguably most of all because of the sort of man he was and the sort of things he believed and preached. This is an account of how a quintessentially non-Christian, or anti-Christian, man became respected in his lifetime and has managed to retain that respect ever since. As such it is a tale for our own times. How many HG Wells types are still with us today, and still doing rather well?

Wells

As Christians we are on the front line of defence against what is known as social engineering. We believe that people are made by God, in His image. As such they cannot be treated as goods, used as victims in some bizarre experiment. Whilst we welcome medical progress and technical advances, we know that science can be used for immoral as well as moral ends.

The work and results of social engineering are seen regularly today, but social engineering itself is nothing new. Let us go back sixty years to a leafy European suburb. A group of men gather around the table and share a joke about one of their colleagues. He is the only one amongst them who isn't a man of science, isn't a doctor. He is a handsome man, with his blonde hair, blue eyes and carved features. Gifted too, and the head of state's favourite politician. But he simply isn't one of them. They have spent years at various universities studying chemistry, biology, physics and the related disciplines that compose the magnificent world in which they place so much hope. They are pioneers, knights of progress, disciples of the scientific muse.

Because they are rooted in science, soaked in its genius, they know that whatever they think and say is wise and, more than this, ethical. Science has to be ethical because it represents the future and the future has to be better than the past. Simple logic. I breathe therefore I am. The arrogance of the living. The dictatorship of chronology. So they discuss, drink coffee, smile and come to a unanimous conclusion about what they must do.

The handsome rival was SS Commander Reinhard Heydrich, the head of state was Adolf Hitler and this was the Wannsee Conference, in which the Final Solution of the "Jewish problem" was decided upon and planned. Men of science could find no moral objection to what they were about to do. And frankly, I am not particularly surprised.

Fast-forward to the present and a good, gentle, caring man who would shudder at the thought of Nazism and death camps walks into a small room in a hospital and sits down next to a pretty young woman. She is pregnant, was happy beyond belief but is now frightened. She can see on the doctor's face that something is wrong. He explains to her that the tests have revealed that her child, if born, would not be, well, would not be normal. He gives his best "I know how you feel" look and explains that science is a wonderful things. She does not have to proceed with the pregnancy. Interestingly enough he starts to use scientific language. Her baby is no longer a baby, it is now a fetus. Science, he says, can give you a choice.

Actually he is right. Science has given us a choice, but it is choice without responsibility. Now I am not for a moment making a qualitative comparison between a Nazi warlord and a contemporary obstetrician. I am simply saying that the more we can do because of the expansion of science, the more we should root ourselves in an unchanging moral code. But we don't.

Simply because we "can" do certain things does not mean that we "should" do them. Not a week goes by without another aspect of scientific capabilities clashing with existing virtues. Sex-change operations, so-called population control, chemical contraceptives, genetic experiments. We look up as children in a planetarium, fascinated and excited but terribly confused. We look for a hand to hold but there is nobody there. And the culture tells us not to worry, merely to trust in science and leave the morals to the men in white coats.

What is so extraordinary about all this is that the father of the whole enterprise, the whole notion of rule by science, was in fact a short, plump Englishman with a high-pitched voice and a bad moustache. H.G. Wells is better known for writing science fiction novels such as *The Invisible Man, The Time Machine* and *The War of the Worlds* than for changing the world. But not only in his scientific politics but also in his greater attitudes and opinions Wells was in many ways the very first modern man. So welcome to the world of H.G. Wells.

There is an anecdote about Wells that exemplified his character more than a dozen memoirs. The bar of a London theatre in the 1920s. Herbert George Wells, a literary doyen of the greatest celebrity, when that really meant something, sips a blended brandy. A breathless young student approaches Wells, holds out his hand and exclaims, "Mr. Wells, you probably don't remember me ..." "Yes I bloody well do" replies Wells, and runs from the theatre.

Rude, nasty, selfish. Yet since his death in 1946 Wells has been treated rather kindly by biographers, rather too kindly. He was a bully who wanted to use science to control the world, he was a bitter anti-Semite, he was a misogynist who treated women in an appalling fashion and he was a racist whose ideas of human experimentation were personally absorbed by Hitler, Stalin and the generations of social engineers who followed them.

There are several reasons why Wells has got away with it for so long. The first is that as a man who was dedicated to science and progress he could apparently do no wrong. The second is that he was a socialist, and we all know that it is only people on the right who are capable of being blackguards, don't we. The third is that a great many people of influence agreed and agree with him. For example, Wells wanted to strictly control the "breeding" of people of colour in Africa and Asia. Imagine that. Yet today Western governments will only give aid to such countries if they agree to allow widespread abortion and promote contraception. So very different? I can't see it. Remember that we could feed these people twice over and not even notice any financial hardship.

The dramatist George Bernard Shaw knew Wells for many years. Describing his ideas and behaviour he wrote:

Multiply the total by ten; square the result. Raise it again to the millionth power and square it again; and you will still fall short of the truth about Wells—yet the worse he behaved the more he was indulged; and the more he was indulged the worse he behaved.

Shaw, however, was something of a friend who killed with kindness. Hilaire Belloc, that champion of Catholicism, was more direct. "Mr. Wells means to say all that is in him, and if there is not very much in him, that is not his fault." It is hardly surprising that Belloc was an enemy, but it is extremely surprising that so many feminists have adored Wells down the ages. From his contemporaries, to the mothers of Planned Parenthood, and even to modern feminist writers, Wells is treated as a hero. His book *Ann Veronica* was and still is considered a seminal work. Indeed it is in print precisely because of the devotion of Britain's largest feminist publishing house.

"The thing to do is to go out into the world; leave everything behind, wife and child, and things; go all over the world and come back experienced," he announced to a group of friends one evening. One onlooker asked what would happen to the wives. "The wives will go to heaven when they die," he said. Wells did not believe in heaven.

Such were Wells' own domestic arrangements. When Amy Catherine Robbins married Wells she was told by her husband that she would have to change her name. Not only her surname. Her Christian name was not to Wells' liking and from now on she would be called Jane. She acquiesced, partly because she knew that Wells would leave her if she resisted and partly because of the undoubted hold he had over women. Lots of them.

Rebecca West was a leading feminist of her age. She was forced to leave London when she gave birth to Wells' illegitimate child because the presence of the boy might embarrass his father. West was both emotionally and physically abused by her "lover" and was frequently publicly humiliated by him when he would shout and laugh at her in crowded restaurants and explain to people at adjacent tables that his mistress had grown ugly. He even had his wife referee between rival mistresses, forcing her to decide with whom he should next be unfaithful.

Another woman, Hedwig Verena Gatternigg, attempted suicide in Wells' front room and he spent more time in trying to keep the story out of the press than in trying to save her life. Amber Reeves, a young and innocent woman, was violated by Wells and then left to take care of her pain and her child. "For all my desire to be interested I have to confess that for most things and people I don't give a damn," he wrote in his autobiography.

He did care about Jews. "I met a Jewish friend of mine the other day and he asked me what would come of his people," Wells wrote. "That is exactly what is the matter with them—my people." That man's people were about to be exterminated in The Holocaust. Writing of The First World War Wells stated:

> *Throughout those tragic and almost fruitless four years of war, the Jewish spokesmen were most elaborately and energetically demonstrating that they cared not a rap for the troubles and dangers of English, French, Germans, Russians, Americans or of any other people but their own. They kept their eyes steadfastly upon the restoration of the Jews.*

It was pointed out to Wells that the first volunteer for the American forces in Europe was Jewish, that there were numerous Jewish winners of the Iron Cross, that Jews were in fact over-represented in the fighting armies. His response was sullen aggression.

There was never a promise; they were never chosen; their distinctive observances, their Sabbath, their Passover, their queer calendar, are mere traditional oddities of no present significance whatsoever.

Eleanor Roosevelt called Wells a fool and a bigot and tried to have him banned from the U.S.A. Leon Gelman, President of the Mizrachi Organization of America wrote at the time:

Wells is brazenly spreading notorious lies about the Jews. His violent language betrays a streak of sadism that is revolting. If any man who professes to be an enlightened human being can preach such heinous distortions, then mankind is doomed to utter darkness.

Quite so.

Which leads us to Wells the social engineer. In massively best selling books such as *Anticipations* and *A Modern Utopia* Wells wrote that he believed the world would collapse and from this collapse a new order should and would emerge.

People throughout the world whose minds were adapted to the big-scale conditions of the new time. A naturally and informally organized educated class, an unprecedented sort of people.

A strict social order would be formed. At the bottom of it were the base.

These were "people who had given evidence of a strong anti-social disposition," including "the black, the brown, the swarthy, the yellow." Christians would also "have to go" as well as the handicapped. Wells devoted entire pamphlets to the need of "preventing the birth, preventing the procreation or preventing the existence" of the mentally and physically handicapped.

> *This thing, this euthanasia of the weak and the sensual is possible. I have little or no doubt that in the future it will be planned and achieved.*

The people of Africa and Asia, he said, simply could never find a place in a modern world controlled by science. Better to do away with them than tell them lies. "I take it they will have to go," he said of them. Marriage as it is known would have to end but couples could form unions based on mutual needs and desires. They would list their "desires, diseases, needs" on little cards and a central authority would decide who was fitted for whom.

Population would be rigidly controlled, with forced abortion for those who were not of the right class and race and a firm control of family size even for the "acceptable" population. Religion would be unnecessary and banned, children would be raised in communes and all would be well. The old and the ill would, naturally, have to be done away with and doctors would be given the authority to decide who had a right to love, who had a duty to die.

Remember that Wells was an internationally best-selling author before television, before radio was popular. He sold literally millions of copies of his books, translated into numerous languages. He was a star of his age, and he dominated the literary and cultural world from as early as 1900, right up until the Second World War. His warning of the horror of future air-war, for example, is thought by historians to have made a huge contribution to Britain's reluctance to rearm against Germany in the 1930s.

Stalin knew of Wells' importance and relished his work. He met with Wells and enjoyed the encounter so much that he cancelled the rest of the day's activities so he could listen to the great man for even longer. Hitler thought that Wells spoke and wrote for the "new man" and should be listened to by the modern world.

Wells was pleased at this adulation and continued to write about his favourite subject, about the future and how it should develop. In his *The Outline of History* he offered similar views, but perhaps didn't do all of the work himself. During the writing of the book he delivered a lecture to a group of young people. One of them inquired about a folder of papers in Wells' car. "Today I've motored from Stonehenge, and you may care to know that I've polished that off in forty minutes." The student was surprised, reminding Wells that Stonehenge had baffled experts of hundreds of years.

Very likely, but anyway I've settled it to my satisfaction. I've left a couple of experts behind, they have a fussy kind of knowledge that looks well in a footnote.

In other words he was a plagiarist. Other people were doing the work for him and he was taking the credit and the cash. I suppose we should not be surprised. What should surprise us is the lasting influence of man who is not really read any more. People who couldn't name a book by Wells have been raised in a context and an environment where his ideas are increasingly acceptable. He was an authentic man of vision. He influenced the future, and he described the future. Vision indeed. Trouble is, it is a dark and horrible vision that comes into sharper focus by the day.

ON CONSERVATISM

*T*his is one essay, one attempt to outline a Christian approach to conservatism. As I have said elsewhere in this book, concepts of left and right are increasingly redundant and increasingly troublesome for the politically active Christian. But if we are to operate in the real world of government and ideas we will, inevitably, be faced with such ideas. Thus my offering, my challenge to those who might feel just a little too comfortable with a single political party of political ideology.

Conservative

Many Christians regard themselves as being conservatives. I am increasingly uncomfortable with any label other than Christian, but as Christians we are called upon not only to be shaped by God but also to live in the practical world.

As such, some of our struggles on moral issues will, whether we like it or not, involve us in conservative movements. Thus we have to work out, perhaps with fear and trembling, what we mean by social conservative. And be very careful indeed that we do not become entangled in a very different, and arguably far less Christian, sense of conservatism.

There is no explicit and distinct credo around which social conservatives gather but there are certain principles and unchanging ideas and ideals which help to illuminate social conservatism.

These consist of a belief that the family and the community, rather than the individual, is the basis of society and that without strong families and the legal and constitutional defence of the same, society will disintegrate. A belief that the ideal and natural family is composed of a man and a woman and their children. A belief that single parent families do of course occur and while capable of being vital and valid units, often involving heroic sacrifice, are not desirable and should not be seen in any way as an ideal. A belief that same-sex couples, while they must be respected, do not constitute families and that when science is exploited to give such people children it is the wrong and immoral use of science. A belief that marriage can only be between a man and a woman. A belief that life begins at conception and ends at natural death and that abortion is the taking of the life of a pre-born or un-born child. A belief that euthanasia is unacceptable, no matter how compassionate some people allegedly and wrongly think it to be. A belief that the state has not only a right but a duty to intervene in some areas of personal life. Censorship of pornography, for example, is a valid expression of government, as is the control of prostitution or of certain forms of hateful speech.

A belief that economic freedom, while desirable, does not necessarily guarantee a good and fair society and is not an end in itself nor, in a moral vacuum, even a means to an end. A belief that any nation-state has a responsibility to guard its borders and that while immigration is essential and valuable it may, must, also be controlled. The needs of the host population as well as the potential citizen must be taken into account, and while compassion must always be a key factor in deciding who is allowed into a country, it is vital that the needs of that nation's economy are taken into account. A state also has the right to guarantee that newcomers are not criminals, are prepared to work and observe the manners of the nation. While issues of colour, race and religion are irrelevant, issues of national commitment and respect for democracy, family and the rule of law are vital. Countries have identities, and must be more than a collection of economically profitable shopping-malls. A belief that while the individual has a fundamental right to be free, he has to be free within the limits of an ethical society and that freedom must not infringe on that of others. The freedom, for example, to use illegal drugs or to promote violence is not freedom at all but glorified selfishness. A belief that we do not live in splendid isolation but in far more splendid union with others.

A belief that while not every citizen believes in God, organized religion and the Judeo-Christian concepts that formed modern Europe and North America must be respected and honoured and that we are all products of natural law and directly influenced by its ramifications. A belief that tradition is a binding, unifying and positive force and that faith, honour, duty, authority and patriotism are constants. A belief in equality under the law, irrespective of race, gender or religion. A belief that while human beings are capable of noble, great and even angelic acts their natures are not perfect and often have to be controlled by the state. A belief that a democratically elected government, supported by an independent judiciary, is the only legitimate body that can form laws and exercise state authority.

Some of these issues have become particularly divisive both within the conservative movement and outside of it. Abortion, for example, is a subject that splits the conservative movement to a profound extent. Some neo-conservatives and many others simply cannot understand what all the fuss is about. They believe that life begins only at birth and that it makes economic sense to control the population.

They also see the issue as a digression from matters fiscal. If, as the vast majority of social conservatives believe, abortion is nothing less than the killing of a child the issue can be nothing other than central and the battle never-ending. To ask a social conservative, a pro-lifer, to bend and adapt on the subject of abortion would be like asking any other man to not mind so much about the beheading of his mother or, more exactly, the genocide of an entire people. It is an issue that cannot be over-stated because it is an issue of life and death. In comparison, levels of taxation and notions of free trade do tend to diminish in importance.

The social conservative belief is based on a massive support of evidence, research and argument. It runs as follows. It is a proven fact that human life begins at conception and there can be no other starting-point. Apart from anything else, a baby is genetically complete at conception. The child's heart is beating by the 25th day and three days later its legs, arms, eyes and ears are already beginning to form. The child's brain has distinctly human features by this period. The first bone cells appear in the sixth week and begin to replace the cartilage of the already complete skeleton. The child's milk teeth begin to form in the following week. By this time its fingers, thumbs, ankles and toes have also begun to form. By the tenth week all the child's limbs and organs are established and it can turn its head, bend its elbows and wrists and even make facial gestures such as frowning. The child is also - and this is extremely important - sensitive to touch. This is now quite obviously a human being, even to the layman's eye. By the twelfth week the child can swallow, its fingernails have started to grow and its ribs and vertebrae have become bone. The child's vocal chords are complete and its reproductive organs are well advanced. Inherited physical features can also be discerned at this stage - the child looks like its father or mother. At sixteen weeks it is half its birth length and its heart pumps at the rate of about fifty pints a day. Eyebrows and eyelashes have begun by the fifth month and the child now turns, kicks and sucks its thumb. The birth of the child four months later is simply an incident in an already advanced process.

As a pro-life pamphlet had it:

> *If it is wrong to kill a child at birth it must be wrong to kill him at 28 weeks, sixteen weeks, twelve weeks, eight weeks, four weeks. Human life is human life is human life. It is entirely arbitrary to pick a moment and say: now he's human, before that he wasn't. Human development is a continuous process, a steady 'becoming', from conception onwards.*

This is true for an unborn advocate of abortion as much as it is for an unborn advocate of life.

The issue of homosexuality is another subject that polarises countries and, as such, conservatives within those countries. Many in the conservative movement have been caught up in the essentially liberal and modernistic concept of toleration. They are convinced that a good person is a tolerant person and a very good person is an extremely tolerant person. I tolerate therefore I am.

A tolerance of differing opinions or of a different religion is, of course, absolutely essential and an indication of civilization. Indeed social conservatism regards such tolerance as an essential foundation. But the modern world has reinterpreted tolerance to mean something entirely different—the refusal to pass an opinion and to discern the difference between right and wrong, to indulge in moral equivalents. Ironically, when social conservatives do express their opinions about what is right and wrong they are attacked and abused by "tolerant" liberals as being "intolerant."

For some neo-conservatives the argument over homosexuality goes further. As they believe that every person is primarily an economic unit their sexual activity is really quite irrelevant. Many social conservatives, on the other hand, believe that we are creatures, made with a specific purpose and intended to follow a specific way of life. Homosexuality, while to be tolerated in an open and free society, is not to be encouraged or treated on an equal footing with heterosexuality. Man and woman are more, much more, than the sum of their economic worth. Procreation is not the sole purpose of marriage but it is a crucial one. If homosexuals can be married to each other, why not brothers and sisters, parents and children? It is also naive and disingenuous to argue that if homosexual couples are acknowledged by the state, and by some anti-Christian churches, as being married, it does not alter life for the majority of people. Such an act directly dents the importance and validity of authentic, heterosexual marriage. The actions of the individual affect more than the individual who takes the action and the individuals around them. These actions also effect the entire community.

Then we have the issues of pornography and censorship. These are subjects that, like rocks thrown into a conservative pool, send out ripples in all directions. Many conservatives are reluctant to indulge in censorship, believing that in a perfect world the individual should be allowed complete freedom of expression and freedom to read. This was a tenable position at one time but, I believe, no longer. As social conservatives themselves are repeatedly told, times do change. A 1914 pacifism in the face of the Kaiser's foolishness, for example, would be completely different from a 1939 pacifism in the face of the Führer's Nazism. While opponents of censorship delight in mocking the rather absurd banning of books such as *Lady Chatterly's Lover* or even the delightful Tintin cartoons, they fail or refuse to look at the current situation.

Take, for example, the case of Dennis Cooper, a writer highly regarded in some circles. He is championed by many as just the sort of author the state has no right to regulate. Let us take one of his stories, a work entitled *Frisk*. I must, by the way, warn people at this point that what follows is difficult to read, deeply repugnant and not to be seen by young people. The paradox of my position, however, is that without describing in some way the horrors of these stories I cannot convey just how dreadful they are. But do please be aware.

In *Frisk* a man is murdered for sexual kicks, he is humiliated and hit, he is tortured, and his rectum is used for gruesome and grotesque purposes. "He opened his eyes very wide," writes Cooper. "Otherwise he didn't fight me at all. It takes a lot longer to strangle someone than you'd think." The victim is fifteen.

Or, from the same piece, an account of the rape, sexual beating, and murder of a boy whose excrement the author has just eaten. The victim's penis is cut in two and he is decapitated. The narrator masturbates over this. Friends arrive. "They kicked the corpse around for a while. This created a pretty hilarious fireworks display of blood." Or how about a repugnantly graphic story by one Ann Wertheim about incestuous rape. In this elaborately constructed lesbian fantasy the victim is shown as enjoying herself as she welcomes agonizing penetration, oral sex and physical violence from her father.

Both of these stories appeared in a book entitled *Forbidden Passages*. Of the last piece, one of the compilers of the anthology wrote that when it came into her office "several of us nearly fainted from intense levels of sexual heat." Now imagine if we read of a group of Klansmen describing the beating, torture and murder of a black teenager, with graphic detail and description, and then read in an introduction to a collection of banned writings that one of the editorial staff almost fainted over this particular story because of the racist passion in the office. Both involve an innocent, bewildered victim, both involve breaking both the moral and the civil law and both would be anathema to societal standards.

With hate literature, Holocaust denial, and the like, we can at least defeat these rancid ideas with simple fact. But the literary depiction of sadistic pedophilia and the sexual torture of children is not about fact but about a basic immoral stance. This is much harder to control, partly because these things involve intellectual as well as physical masturbation. But none of us, surely, still believe that there is no link between pornography and crime.

The questions often asked are, Where do we draw the line? and, Who is to do the drawing? The answers are not as complex as some would have us believe, and need not be extreme or even noticeable to the overwhelming majority of people. We draw lines of limitation every day and give politicians, judges, police officers and teachers the authority to use ethical pencils. Individual customs officers, overworked and underqualified, are not the most suitable guardians of our literary borders, but there is no reason why a panel of judges should not decide on what is allowed to enter the country. We allow, after all, such a system to control the flow of people into various countries and it is surely axiomatic that one book is capable of much more harm than a single man or woman. Conservatism is a living ideology and as such it has to be able to adapt and to change, without losing sight and sound of its essentials.

It is also about practicality and about practical politics. Its oxygen is reality. It was and is produced by the world and the world's events; unlike other political beliefs, conceived only to shape the world and the world's events. It reacts to reality, as it did to the summer of 1997 in North America. This was not a peculiar season, not an extraordinary season, not an atypical season in the continent's history. We could probably take any few months from the last ten years and extract similar events. The summer of 1997 does reveal, however, certain events that illustrate the issues facing and defining contemporary social conservatism.

There was the topless issue, a subject that delighted the headline writers but had a far more significant effect upon society at large. After a series of court decisions and appeals it was decided in Ontario that women should be allowed to go about in public with their breasts exposed. Toplessness was now allowed, on the street as well as on the beach. A group of judges decided that women should be allowed to show their boobs to any boobs who might be interested. This represented a profound change in what society believed to be decent and moral and that very society protested against such change with demonstrations and petitions.

This was also a direct challenge to social conservatives, who see social engineering, the forced and contrived elimination of gender differences and aggressive changes to existing societal standards as a fundamental attack upon society and community. The arguments put forward by the equality fanatics was that because men were permitted to bare their chests women should be allowed the same right. Women's breasts, however, are directly sexual, the second most erogenous part of a woman's body, and are also more biologically intimate in that they are used for nursing children. Also, only certain types of men would walk along the streets topless, because a thin T-shirt prevents sunburn and may deflect heat. Be they the owners of beer-bellies of perfect pectorals, those men who want to show their upper bodies to the greater world are usually making a deeper, more neurotic point. We should be dissuading them, not persuading others.

The only generally acceptable form of exposure is during nursing, when we should encourage women to feed their children whenever and wherever they want. Breast-feeding represents much of what is best about humanity, such as love, procreation and family. But the so-called Breast-Walkers' reasoning represented the precise opposite of the nursing scenario and their behaviour is the contrary of natural. It is full not of care and bonding, but of egotism and perversity.

Which brings us back to the great modern myth of tolerance, the great bullying chimera of the social conservative.

Because the legal blessing of toplessness was seen as being tolerant it was welcomed by some as a progressive action. Social conservatism, ever pragmatic, should ask two questions: How many of these people would feel comfortable conducting a conversation with a 70-year-old lady who had her breasts exposed, and how many of them would allow their children to be taught by a bare-breasted woman? Defenders of the decision also argued that few women would take advantage of the ruling anyway. If that was the case, there was no need to alter a fundamental of society. It is true that no emotionally, sexually and politically mature woman would expose herself in public but equally true that some politically extreme women are not particularly mature.

The freedom of a small group of people to do what is contrary to the dictates and history of civilized society now overwhelms the freedom of the majority. A restaurant is crowded with families. One woman enters, swinging her exposed breasts. She is indeed free to act in such a manner. And as a consequence every person in that room has to explain to their children, justify to themselves, change their values and virtues, leave the restaurant. This is not liberty but licence.

At around the same time that the courts were making a mountain out of something, well, something much smaller there came a fine decision by The Supreme Court that the act of lap-dancing was indecent. This made it much easier for the police to ban such activities and arrest those involved. Here was morality meeting the free market, the social conservative meeting his neo-con brother.

The latter argued that individuals have the right to do what they want with their own bodies and that the free market is sacred and lap-dancing is merely a form of financial transaction. They also stated that the court had enforced a particular morality when morals are not universal.

The social conservative response is that lap-dancing involves several people. The man paying the money, the woman dancing, the club owner and the rest of us who make up general society. The man with the cash may, after the court's decision, have his freedom restricted, but not so the dancer. There are very few women who willingly prostitute themselves, but many who do so out of economic desperation. A single mother in near poverty is not acting from her own free will. Nor is she free to choose where she dances. Any club owner knows that if a neighbouring venue offers lap-dancing, he will have to follow suit to maintain his clientele. Men will not patronize a non-touching club if there is a full contact one down the road. Thus, a dancer no longer has any choice. She was uneasy with stripping, but at least she was not mauled. Before lap-dancing became common she could retain a modicum of dignity by merely dancing or stripping on stage.

As for the wider community, I have yet to hear any convincing argument that our physical, spiritual, ethical or educational well-being is in any way improved by allowing lap-dancing. I have, however, heard many arguments that permitting such an indulgence eats away at the very core of our society. There is such a thing as collective responsibility.

Then come the arguments concerning the free market. For a market to be genuinely free, the participants must enjoy something like equal rights and privileges. A union stranglehold or a business monopoly prevents true economic liberty. So what of the pimps, pushers, bouncers and brutal club owners? Indeed a former lap-dancer said after the court decision that the clubs will now be free of "the pigs and the prostitutes." To assume that a dancer is able to choose her place of work and her working conditions and is able to keep an equitable share of the evening's proceeds is laughable.

Those who are so concerned with the free market would do well to read the arguments of those men in the last century who employed 10-year-old chimney-sweeps. They said the boys were not being forced into the work and that the lads were paid and cared for. Because the society of the time had less refined and sensitive views toward child labour it accepted such a defence. Yet when reformers educated that society, the arguments of the child exploiters suddenly blew away like dirty ashes.

The same will happen if, and when, we educate our society about the reality of lap-dancing, sexual commercialism and its ethical consequences. The state has a right to limit and control the outer limits of the market so such a market can be, in the most authentic sense, truly free.

Last comes the issue of morality. We impose something like a universal morality a great deal of the time, precisely because it is considered universal. Those who argue that the state has no right to decide what is right and wrong put themselves in a contradictory position. They come to their conclusions in the first place solely because they themselves have their own theories of right and wrong and, consequently, impose them on the state and its decisions. If there is no such entity as universal morality there can be no such thing as conservatism. We cannot conserve what is not at least largely static in its fundamental ethical framework. What is extraordinary about the world is not how many moral codes have existed down the ages but how few there have been. Agreement on the essentials is almost unanimous.

As all this was going on, Gay Pride Week was celebrated. Social conservatives have been extraordinarily accepting over the past decade in accommodating extremist challenges from homosexual groups. This particular celebration of the homosexual sub-culture, however, went beyond anything seen in the past. A police officer announced that he was disturbed by the men in the Gay Pride parade who marched along the streets with their genitals exposed, with pierced testicles on display or who took part in acts of sadomasochistic sex. In what seemed like an eminently reasonable statement the officer concluded that

> *It just seems to be escalating past the point of fair play and common decency. We're certainly concerned. If this type of thing happens next year, we'll stop the parade.*

But the good sergeant was wrong. In fact the police were not concerned by all these acts of flagrant law-breaking. Within 24 hours, in a series of statements from police headquarters, it was announced that the Deputy Chief had "no problems with the parade," that the parade would definitely continue, that a debriefing meeting would be held "but the issue of nude revellers" would not be discussed and, in what must be a quote to put in the record books, that it was doubtful whether "concerns over some male parade-goers exposing their genitals will even be raised."

That the law was broken was beyond doubt. There was and is a great deal of footage of naked men strolling around in the parade, of acts of indecent exposure and of bondage and whipping. What was extraordinary was how quickly and how vehemently the bureaucrats and high-ranking officers in the police department contradicted a front-line officer and how eager they were to excuse the law-breakers

Yet Gay Pride organizers seemed willing to make no such changes. One of them said that the "bondage floats" and the nudity were "quite tame and that he did not find them to be "unacceptable." So now a special interest group spokesman shapes what is permissible and thus what is the law for the rest of society. Homosexual activists frequently try to change the laws to accommodate or protect their own ways of life. That is their right. It is significant, though, that while they want the majority of the population to accept such new laws many homosexual radicals seem intent on mocking and breaking the laws that already accommodate and protect that same majority.

The counter to any such arguments is to scream out accusations about homophobia, a contrived and meaningless word invariably used to silence free debate. But the debate must continue. If a section of society wants to change a country so radically that public sex and genital exhibitionism are standard, let them at least be honest about it. A single person walking along the street without any clothes would be stopped and, if necessary, arrested. Two heterosexuals whipping each other's semi-naked bodies in the middle of a city would, again, be stopped and, if necessary, arrested. The law must apply equally to all, otherwise it is no law at all.

Much of all this concerns how we perceive the nature of state, government and authority. A healthy fear and mistrust of the state is surely a good thing and something all conservatives should cultivate. But they should also understand the difference between gratuitous state intervention and essential government regulation. Social conservatism accepts the place of the state and sees it not always as a last resort but often as a constructive regulator and intervenor. Consider a group of people playing a team sport. They are given complete freedom, in that there is no referee, no uniforms and no rules. They foul each other, hurt each other, have no idea what is going on and end up fighting. They are truly free but are not truly happy. What should have been a magnificent sport became an ugly mess. Then consider the team sport in which there are too many rules and the referee is officious and intrusive. The sport becomes a slow, muddy annoyance. The participants are neither free nor happy.

There is, however, a middle way. The rules can be applied intelligently and fairly. The referee can be accountable and understanding, the players responsible and, knowing that the referee understands the game, observe the rules. The result is the game as it should be played, with the maximum enjoyment for the maximum number of players. The truly offensive and violent players are taken off. The participants are free in the real sense and happy in a meaningful sense.

The modern state is feared and despised for good reason. It indulges in ludicrous interventions into our daily lives and often seems intent on extending its own power simply for the sake of power itself. But a greater accountability, a change in the electoral process and a more actively political population could change this, without requiring the disappearance of the state itself. For example, there are currently attempts being made in North America to make it a crime for parents to spank their children. An absurd and offensive example of state interference, often initiated by people who do not have any children. But the state already makes it illegal for parents to physically assault their children, which is surely a good thing. It is the nature of the state and the extent of its power, not its very existence, which has to be questioned.

Let us take the case of the late eighteenth-century social conservative and economic interventionist William Wilberforce, a man who understood and appreciated the dynamic between citizen and state. After this politician's conversion to Christianity he gave himself two goals. He dedicated his life to the abolition of slavery, and to reformation of the manners of the English people. By slavery Wilberforce was referring to the wretched kidnapping, sale and slaughter of Africans by the European powers, a trade that injected fortunes into the economies of Britain, France, Spain, Holland and other nations. By manners he meant morality.

It could be argued that slavery would have eventually come to an end because human labour was not as efficient as machinery and the free market would have dictated that the slave trade was unprofitable. This is what some Tory MPs and slave owners argued in the 1790s. But Wilberforce argued that this was most unlikely. He was right. He forced an end to European slavery half a century before Abraham Lincoln's declaration and the American Civil War. Slavery still continues in some places to this day. So slavery did not end due to market forces and the free market can be awfully slow in doing what it does. More than this, however, is the essential humanity of conservatism. It is a politics that demands social action. Slavery could only be abolished by the determined intrusion of the state into the lives of individuals, businesses, communities and even foreign governments. The Royal Navy was obliged to attack foreign slave traders and sometimes kill them. Instead of free trade was fire trade. If you want to be free, we have to fire.

But while Wilberforce spent decades calling for state action against slavery he also called for the state to withdraw from the life of the Christian church and to leave religious non-conformists alone. He argued that the Church of England, the national church, should withdraw from national life and that non-Anglican Christians should be allowed full participation in national affairs, without fear of financial penalty or social stigma. He understood when the state should interfere and when the state should leave alone.

Similarly with the reformation of the country's manners. What we think of as Victorian progress, which ironically enabled the free market and economic expansion to occur, only came about after the transformation of England from its eighteenth-century decadence. Wilberforce the social conservative was an integral part of this process. He preached to individuals and groups but he also lobbied for the government to control the sale of alcohol and to enforce standards in family life.

Another great social conservative, the British journalist and broadcaster Malcolm Muggeridge, once said that "without moral order, a society can have no real order at any level." Now this is interesting. Because many of those who call themselves conservatives and who preach freedom seem to be unaware of this surely self-evident fact. The liberty of the swimmer to float out to sea is actually better known as drowning. There is no example in history of authentic progress without authentic order. Nations and empires were only economically and culturally productive when they were relatively ordered societies, with a suitably strong government. Further, when the moral order of those societies began to decay economic and political collapse quickly followed. The Roman Empire is only one example of this. First came moral disintegration, then political catastrophe, then what we now think of as The Dark Ages.

Many social conservatives believe that a new dark age may be upon us unless we rethink our ways. The state is being used to end human life rather than to save it. It is being used to open our borders to damaging and obscene literature rather than guarding them against such material. Its legal arm appears to be intent on dismantling the civilized order rather than safeguarding it. G.K. Chesterton said that:

> *All conservatism is based upon the idea that if you leave things alone you leave them as they are. But you do not. If you leave a thing alone you leave it to a torrent of change.*

Which is why those in the social conservative movement are intent, in the spirit of true conservatism, on changing much and restoring more. They come not so much to innovate as to renovate. And they must do it now, before it is too late.

ON RELIGION

*S*ome people might not understand why a book about Christianity has a section entitled "On Religion." Is not all of Christianity, they might ask, about religion? I would say not. In fact it seems to me that Christ came to tell us that religion was the last thing we should be concerned about. Not religion, He said, but relationship. Having said that, it is convenient to use a single word to describe the places where the Christian life and relationship meets the general culture. I have used the term religion. Here are various columns about various aspects of a various religious life.

Authors

In early 2002 yet another book was published attacking Jesus, the Christian story and, by extension, anyone foolish enough to believe that Jesus was born to a virgin, was the Messiah and son of God, died for our sins and rose again. The fact that many of the greatest minds in history have believed this seems to escape so many modern novelists and critics.

The book in question made little impact in North America or Europe, but it is interesting in that it represented a whole wave of such efforts, both in fiction and non-fiction. Having said this though, it does not mean that Christians should shy away from current literature and hide ourselves away in our own sub-culture. Far from it. We have to show the world that we have something better to offer.

There is currently a great deal of heat over a book called *Testament* by Canadian author Nino Ricci. The novel concerns the life of Jesus, as told by four different people. And, what a surprise, it is intended to shock. Jesus wasn't the person we thought, we are told. He was conceived by a Roman soldier who raped His mother, He wasn't the Messiah, and so on.

All the sort of stuff that is published in fiction and in sloppy non-fiction books every year. Which is why I cannot quite understand how this book is supposed to be so controversial and why it's receiving so much ink. It's all been said before. But Jesus still lives, and all His critics are dust, mere food for worms.

I have met Nino Ricci several times and he seems like a very nice guy. Nor have I ever heard anything to the contrary. Whether he is a swine or a sweetheart, however, is not the issue. If I am to criticize the book as a Christian, I must also criticize its author as a Christian. In other words, not really criticize him at all. Love you Nino, but I think you've got it wrong with this one.

The first thing we should establish is how fortunate we all are to be writing in a culture based on Christian ideals. This is precisely what gives Ricci, amongst others, the freedom to be so provocative and offensive to so many people. It is almost redundant now to remind everyone that such a book could not be written in a Moslem state.

More than this, the Soviets banned books that dealt harshly with anyone of whom Moscow disapproved and even tortured the books' authors. The same happens now in China. Atheist regimes are notoriously intolerant. In fact the only cultures where concepts of literary and artistic freedom have flourished are those founded on the teachings of Christ.

So it's ironic then, but undeniable, that Ricci has a perfect right to pen such a book. But I do wish he'd given us something new. Goodness me, does he really think that such attacks have not been made in the past? Ancient Jewish scholars accused Jesus of being the child of a woman raped by a Roman soldier. The myth continued even to, well, even to Monty Python and The Life of Brian.

First-century graffiti shows Christians as being oxen. In other words, dumb and stupid. Other wall drawings from the time have followers of Jesus drinking blood and eating flesh. Indeed this is still believed in some countries. We have always been targets and victims. Hey, it was supposed to be that way. No surprise, surely, that those who live in the light are so despised by those who find comfort in the darkness.

There will be some Christians, naturally, who will become very angry about the book and call for it to be banned. They may well embarrass themselves because they haven't read it but claim to know its contents. So what. Righteous anger is understandable and we all make mistakes. But the reaction of a minority is less important than the smugness that produced the book in the first place.

In 2002, seventeen Indonesian Christians were hacked to death by Moslem fanatics. One of the victims was a tiny baby, its body so torn apart by the blows of the machete that is was almost beyond recognition. Most newspapers ignored the massacre, a handful gave the story a few words.

In the Middle East, a young man even now sits in a prison cell praying. His crime is that he is a convert to Yeshua, Jesus. The very saviour Nino Ricci so mocks. This Christian has already been whipped and may well face execution. He will be merely the latest in a whole chain of recent martyrs.

It would be nice, just once, if some of those who think it dangerous and daring to throw stones at those they know will not fight back, would embrace the real issues, take on the genuine evil of the world. Otherwise they seem a little irritating but, more to the point, utterly irrelevant. Which could never be said of Jesus Christ, Lord of the world.

Unique

I wasn't sure whether to write this one or not. Sometimes it's best to simply leave a subject alone, wait for the fog of ignorance to evaporate. But there just has to be comment this time. The issue is that of religion, and the attacks on it in the media since the tragedy of September 11. The thesis is that all religions are the same, they all produce hatred and violence, and that the world would be a better place without them.

What has to be stated immediately is that the greatest violence in terms of numbers of victims and intensity of sadism has come not from those professing religion but those claiming the contrary. It was the twentieth-century, the great age of atheism and materialism, that saw the real mass murderers take the stage. The regimes of Hitler, Stalin, Mao, Pol Pot and their other social engineer friends had in common a detestation of religious faith and a belief that God was dead.

Man makes his own morality, they argued, and there was no need to listen to any pretend creator or judge. They then promptly murdered hundreds of millions of people.

Suddenly any ignorant religious fanatic of the past was made to look the amateur he really was.

Which is to say that yes, of course, religion has been used for all sorts of things. How could it not be? People use love, family, country, freedom, race, anything as a means to go to war or steal or lie. That religion should be similarly exploited should come as no surprise to anyone who properly understands the world and its inhabitants.

Yet what religion, specifically Christianity, also does is to raise billions of dollars to give to the needy while governments attach sometimes punitive conditions to their aid. It establishes health care and education when the secular state is different. It sends doctors, engineers, farmers into war zones and slums ignored by the rest of the world.

The war against slavery, the campaign against child labour, redistribution of wealth, social equality, are all Christian concepts and constructs. Easy now to mock Christian people who sometimes do not present their causes with the utmost skill or eloquence, but surely more witty and graceful to understand how we came to live in a free society than enables us to be so mocking.

Yes, a free society. The very notions of pluralism and modern democracy are products of Christianity, especially in its post-medieval Protestant form. The ideals of tolerance and free expression did not suddenly materialize but evolved out of a belief system based on love and understanding. It is surely no coincidence that what we think of as the free world, whatever its problems, is also the world established on Christian principles.

I mention Christianity because it is my faith and also, perversely, because it is the religion that is currently being so attacked by people claiming that all religion is bad. These pundits avoid Islam because it is culturally and politically discreet to do so; they don't attack Judaism because they fear being branded as anti-Semites; they fail to mention Hinduism and Buddhism because, in all honesty, they don't really know what they are.

So they settle for good old Christian-bashing. Fair enough, we were told to expect it and it puts us in some pretty good company. But please, don't tell us that all religions are the same. This is like saying that all politics are the same. Try telling that to someone looking down the gun of a fascist soldier.

Christianity is unique because, ironically, it has answers to horrors like September 11. It tells us that revenge solves nothing, that death is not the end, that even evil people are capable of change, that there is absolute truth, that there is a right and wrong, and that no matter how much His creatures might kick and scream and deny, God most certainly does exist.

I have a very strong feeling that at the time of their greatest fear many of the victims of coal black September 11th knew that truth very well. It's not religion that's to blame but humanity's failure to live by it. Don't condemn the law because your break its rules.

Influence

George was only nineteen when he first saw action in North Africa. This night was brutal and the Germans were closing in fast. A shell landed close. Yet why could he not hear anything. Suddenly words spun through the fog that seemed to engulf him and he realized that people were shouting. His best friend, Frank, was asking him something. Then the words made sense. "You've been hit, you've been hit. Can you hear me?"

George looked down to where his legs should have been. No pain, no fear, just a strange clarity. "Frank, you must do something for me." Anything, his friend replied. "Go to Mr. Norbert Johnson in my hometown. Tell him that now it all makes sense. Now I understand and I know it is all true. Please buddy, do it." And then George died. In the middle of a vast desert, a very long way from home.

Frank arrived home, found the right address. A knock on the door. No answer. Another knock. Slowly a figure approached. An elderly man, bending with the burden of the years.

"Mr. Norton Johnson?" Yes, I am. "Mr. Johnson, I'm

not really very good at this, but I have some bad news to give you."

The two men went into the house and sat down. "I'll get straight to the point. George Petersfield was my friend. He was killed in action earlier this year. He insisted that I see you and tell you that 'it all made sense now, that he understood and that it was all true'. That was all, just that."

The old man's face became pale. He asked for the name to be repeated. "George Petersfield. He said it all made sense, that it was all true."

At which the old man began to cry. "Yes, I remember young Georgie," he said, mopping the tears that bisected his craggy face. "I remember the little guy. I didn't think he listened to a word I said."

A pause. "God forgive me, I thought that for all these years I'd been a failure. You see, I was George's teacher, and I'm a Christian. I tried to show him the truth, in small and subtle ways. I thought I'd let him down, let God down." Then a flood of tears.

Simply, we have more influence than we know. More than this, we are called to influence those who seem to be, perhaps, indifferent or even hostile. And none has been more indifferent or hostile than the secular culture in which we find ourselves in contemporary North America. It can seem frightening, dangerous, forbidding. But when we consider further, it's populated by millions of people made by God in His image. Pretty exciting stuff.

Believe me I understand the temptation to remain warm and content within what we know, who we know, where we know. But to do that would be to fall into the trap set by the world. "Keep your religion for Sundays!" Well, it's not a religion at all but a relationship, and to a large extent the last place it should be is in a building on a Sunday morning.

We've all seen those signs on the church door announcing, as we leave, "Welcome to the Mission Field." Not sure if we really believe it. We'll generously donate to Christian work abroad, but seldom speak to our neighbours about the greatest news the world has ever known.

When we do, however, we have to be so careful. "I really appreciate your ministry," "Thank you for sharing your journey," "I'll pray for you" and "I'd like to witness to you." Goodness me, no! Phrases and words that make us feel safe are often anathema to those unused to the Christian world. Indeed, we shouldn't even have a sub-cultural vocabulary. Our job is to be in the world but not of it, meaning we're to be in the middle of it all as a light and a beacon.

If we create an alternative language we alienate. Let me be blunt. How many of you could take a non-Christian friend to church and know that they would feel comfortable? I don't mean made comfortable by the message—God's word must surprise and shock. I mean comfortable in the style and atmosphere. If I hear one more music director telling people, "Put your hands together and clap now," I'll liturgically dance my way out of the building.

What if we don't want to do that, what if we wish to praise God in a different way? Those of us who do are immediately made to feel different, out-of-place. Imagine, then, how a newcomer feels, who may be deeply suspicious of Christians and convinced that everybody is looking at him. We're looking to the unsaved, not those already in His sublime grip.

I'm often asked what it's like working for a non-Christian radio stations and newspapers. The answer is that I behave very much as I do when I work for a Christian television station or as when I write for Christian magazines and publishers. As a result I'm treated fairly. Of course they tease, but that means they're curious.

Pluralism can be terrifying, or it can be wonderful. By the latter I mean that it gives us more opportunities to evangelize than ever before. Of course I wish we still said Merry Christmas instead of Happy Holidays and that prayer wasn't being expunged from public places, but such opposition only gives us more opportunities.

What we had in the past was not as it should have been. So now the whole thing is being shaken around, an experiment in a huge laboratory called pluralism. Secular humanism has had its day and solved nothing. New Age and eastern religion looked appealing but never satisfied. Leaving Him, His life, His death and His words.

It all sounds more like the era of St. Paul than of the 1950s. Know what, I rather like that. I really rather do.

Jewish

I cannot remember being so restless about an international situation. I am a Christian, with three Jewish grandparents. I receive anti-Semitic hate mail every week. To the bigots, my faith in Jesus is not as important as my Jewish blood. This I can tolerate. What I find more troubling is the frequent polarization of Christian opinion on the subject of Israel and Palestine.

For those out there who believe that there is no longer any anti-semitism, the one thing I am sure of is that you are not Jewish. It is seldom to be found in Christian circles, but has regained a foothold elsewhere. To overestimate it would be foolish, but to underestimate would be positively stupid.

I experienced very little anti-semitism growing up. I do remember one occasion when I was only seven or eight years old. I was playing with a boy in the park and, as little boys do, we suddenly became best friends and he invited me back to his house. We played some more. Then his father came in. There was shouting and gesticulation. My new old buddy came up to me. He was obviously upset.

"I'm sorry Mike, but I'm afraid you have to go." He looks to the floor, obviously confused. "My dad says that you have to leave. Sorry."

I left, and couldn't quite understand what had gone on. Perhaps, I thought, I was winning the table soccer game too often. It was only years later that I realized what the father had been shouting. "Is he a Jew, is he a Jew?" The boy said he didn't know; didn't know what a Jew was or whether I was one. "Yes he is, I can tell. Now get him out of here."

So it was. But I survived, and came later in life to know the King of the Jews. I can only hope and pray that the bully of the story made that relationship as well. I do know what happened to his son because I met him many years later. That little boy came to reject his father's racism. At university he met a Jewish girl and they fell in love. After their studies the two got married and had a family. Three children. All Jewish, because their mother was Jewish. How that must have perplexed their grandfather.

In an act of delightful and supernatural completion the couple came to know Jesus Christ, became followers and believers and raised their children as Christians with a strong sense of Jewish identity. They also spend a great deal of their time trying to bring Jewish and Christian people together in a relationship of harmony and love. The perfect answer to darkness.

Today as Christians we also have to avoid darkness, and be able to discuss Israel without fear or prejudice. That is, we must be able to criticize Israeli policies without being accused of anti-semitism. But on the other hand we must only criticize Israeli policies, if that is what we choose to do, if we are free of anti-semitism.

Within the church there is what can be broadly termed the Christian Pacifist approach. Activists are seen on television marching with Palestinians and calling on Israeli soldiers to think again. Fair enough. But they have to understand a few things.

Jews ask where these Christian pacifists were during the Holocaust, when a little over a third of them in Germany actually served in the military. Christians did not, repeat, did not produce the Holocaust. But the Holocaust did occur in what was known as Christendom.

Where, they continue, were the Christian pacifists when 800,000 Jews were thrown out of Egypt, Iraq, Libya, Jordan and elsewhere? The families of these people had lived in the Arab worlds for centuries, but were expelled with only the clothes on their back. Many were killed.

And why, they also ask, are there no Christian pacifists in Syria or Algeria, where Arabs are treated appallingly and slaughtered. An entire village wiped out in the former, hundreds of thousands killed in the latter. Frankly, if a group of eager young people went to these two countries to protest they would not get out again. No media to take pictures, no rule of law, no free courts.

A good, fine Mennonite woman wrote to me recently about Israel. She wrote of Easter, and how peace should descend at such a time. Amen to that. But empathy is vital here. She should know that Easter was traditionally the time of greatest fear for Jewish people in Europe. The local priest would fire up the congregation, and rape, murder and pogrom would result. No young people then standing between Jewish villagers and drunken mobs.

It has become almost fashionable to fly to Israel, drive

to the West Bank and spend a few weeks with a Palestinian family. Then fly home to the suburbs. Perhaps they should spend an evening with what is left of the Koren (Hebrew uses a K) family in Israel, after a dad and two sons were blown to pieces whilst committing the very aggressive act of going to the store to buy some food for the family lunch.

Simply, some people have no safe suburbs to which to return. They want peace, compromise, mutual dignity. But their parents and grandparents went to Israel precisely because Christian Europe tried to eliminate them from the face of the earth.

Yet none of this can allow Israel the right to do whatever it wants. Terrorists must be stopped, but most Palestinians have no link to terror and simply want the same as their Israeli cousins. A safe and free state, self-worth, food and warmth, a future. Because of prophecy, because of the Biblical and moral need for a Jewish homeland, many Christians dehumanize Palestinians. They ought to remember that, apart from anything else, a large number of these people are our brothers and sisters in Christ. Yes, Arabs just like North Americans and Europeans, in relationship with Yeshua, the Jewish Messiah.

A Palestinian Christian friend told me the story of a pastor in the West Bank whose town suddenly came under Israeli fire. He ran with his daughters to a safe place. The girls became hysterical. Sheer terror. When the bombardment stopped the pastor went back to his home and turned on the television. By chance there was an American evangelist interviewing the very same Israeli officer who had been directing the shelling of the pastor's town. The American was, in effect, wishing the Israeli luck in the attack and explaining that American Christians were behind him.

Well they're not. And must not be. They must be behind peace. They must seek to understand both sides, fight anti-semitism as well as anti-Arabism, must look for plausible and genuine alternatives to violence, whomever is the victim. Must pray, must love, must act. Salem, Shalom, Him. Who must be weeping for His beloved homeland.